WALTER PFEIFFER

IN THE HOUSES OF IRELAND

TEXT BY MARIANNE HERON

THAMES AND HUDSON

First published in Great Britain in 1988 by
Thames and Hudson Ltd, London

Published in the United States
by Stewart, Tabori & Chang, Inc.
Photographs copyright © 1988 Walter Pfeiffer
Text copyright © 1988 Marianne Heron

Printed and bound in Japan

For my wife, Valerie, and
my parents

W.P.

For David

M.H.

Acknowledgments

We would like to
thank everyone who has helped us
in the creation of this book, especially those who have been gener-
ous enough to allow the world to
see their homes. We also express
our gratitude to those who gave
invaluable advice, including Alfred
Cochrane, Jeremy Williams, Fergus
Flynn-Rogers, David Slattery (Senior Architect with the Board
of Works), Desmond Fitzgerald
Knight of Glin, John Meagher,
David Sheehan, and Sean Rafferty.
We are indebted for the support
of John O'Connell. Last, but by
no means least, a special thank
you to Roy Finamore, senior editor
at Stewart, Tabori & Chang, who
brought these pages to fruition.

WALTER PFEIFFER AND
MARIANNE HERON

Contents

Author's Note

The living history of houses yields vital clues to the understanding of a land and its people. And in their splendid isolation, Irish houses have evolved without design, so that the evocative layers of the past remain.

I have studied and photographed the vast and richly painted landscape of Ireland for many years. Drawn by a desire to know the secrets of hidden places, I have succumbed to the temptation to follow a winding lane, to ignore a "no trespassing" sign, and wonderful images stay with me. I recall silver light reflected on the windows of a shadowed castle set against the loneliness of dusk. I can see the faintness of blue in the bleached whitewash of a welcoming cottage, steadfast against the everchanging sea. And the warmth of hospitality of a door thrown open to reveal a flagged hall.

In searching for and photographing houses for this book, I have tried to share my experience of this wonderful country. I hope that I have opened doors that will take you into warm rooms made golden by firelight, rooms rich with burgundies or ochres, with the ever Irish green filtering through the windows.

WALTER PFEIFFER

Houses in Town

The locations, names, and layouts of Ireland's towns and cities provide a fascinating insight into their origins. Ireland was originally a pastoral nation with no tradition of urban living; in fact, the only centers of significance were the great monasteries of Ireland's Golden Age of saints and scholars. The Viking invaders founded settlements in the ninth century along the southeast coast in places like Dublin, Limerick, and Waterford, but it was not until the Normans came in 1169 that villages began to be founded in the interior of the country.

Urban development really only got underway in the relative peace of the eighteenth century. Tremendous expansion of provincial towns took place in the early part of the nineteenth century before the disastrous economic effects of the potato famine.

Many of the provincial towns were planned as units, as architecture came to be seen as a way of expressing civic pride. Principal streets were widened, and dignified public buildings, courthouses, town halls, and market houses added as community focal points.

A bit of green behind a Dublin town house.

OPPOSITE: The steep stairwell of a seventeenth-century Dublin house, with a collection of military prints from the South African campaigns. On the left is the Danish flag flown during the Siege of Wood Quay.

Perhaps the best-known example of urban Ireland is Georgian Dublin. In the eighteenth century Dublin was often called the "second city of Europe." The home of the Irish Parliament and the seat of the viceroy, Dublin was a place of significance. Here, influential families acquired elegant town houses in order to pursue their interests close to the source of power. Dublin's Georgian heart was built during the second half of the eighteenth century, the period known as the Irish Renaissance.

Georgian town residences were designed to impress. Some of the interiors are of great elegance, adorned with elaborate plasterwork and with graceful staircases to the principal reception rooms (in earlier houses these were situated on the first floor away from the noise and smell of the street). And though the exteriors of houses changed little between 1730 and 1830, the decorative detail of interiors progressed through a number of styles.

In plasterwork, the straightforward compartmented style of ceiling, with geometric divisions that often disguised beams, gave way by 1740 to elaborate Baroque and Rococo decoration. The Francini brothers, famed Italian stuccodores, introduced the Baroque style to Ireland; they were followed by Irish craftsmen including Robert West, who is particularly noted for the birds he featured in his designs.

After 1760 the work of the British Adam brothers, Robert and James, began to influence design and repetitive neoclassical patterns became fashionable. The best-known Irish stuccodore of this period was Michael Stapleton.

Many of the streets and squares in the center of Dublin owe their layout to the Wide Streets Commission, which was established in 1757. Interestingly, these Georgian streets and squares were not built in an orderly progression, but in a gap-toothed way. Enough ground would be leased for an individual to build two or three houses, one for himself and the others for letting. The interiors of these rented premises were generally made plainer.

Today very few such houses are private residences. Some became tenement dwelling houses; others were converted for use as offices, hotels, or flats. But a few courageous enthusiasts are restoring these houses to their former glory and conserving a threatened aspect of Ireland's heritage.

On this Dublin mantelpiece is a Parian ware piece of Ino and the infant Bacchus after a sculpture by John Henry Foley. The Parian ware piece on the side table is after a sculpture by Patrick MacDowell; the center picture an early eighteenth-century painting of Charity.

The Act of Union in 1800, which abolished the Irish Parliament, brought an end to the expansion of Dublin. Economic decline and famine halted the growth of towns until the Victorian and Edwardian eras. The houses built during these different architectural periods show up like the growth rings on a tree around Irish towns.

These days, the Victorian villas and terraces once built for the expanding middle class and the streets of artisan dwellings have become sought-after homes ripe for gentrification.

The cycle renews itself, as in Joyce's description of Dublin in *Ulysses*: "Cityful passing away, other cityful coming, passing away too: other coming on, passing on."

The Artist's Mews

What is more beautiful in the landscape than a snowy wreath of old [cherry] trees in Spring or more delicate in bud when seen at hand.

WILLIAM ROBINSON, *THE WILD GARDEN*

With changing times the houses in Dublin's grand Georgian squares have become offices and home to corporations. Behind the squares, in a maze of lanes, once-neglected coach houses are being converted to mews cottages, now often lived in by the former occupants of the "big houses."

Standing in a drift of petals under a cherry tree and looking at the blush-pink walls and Gothic-style windows of this cottage, you might suppose that you were in a country retreat. But in fact this secluded mews house is part of one of Dublin's grandest squares, near the heart of the city.

The shell of the building dates to 1810, but there are no traces now of the cobbled floors, stalls, harnesses, and pokey groom's quarters. The mews has been adapted to create a new home for an artist by the Dublin architect Francis Barry.

This is a house with two faces. The front is all whiteness, glass, and seeming modernity; only the large window, which was once the carriage-house door, suggests a former use. To the rear, pink-washed walls and the original pointed Gothic-style windows, which are echoed by a new door leading to the garden, suggest a romantic cottage. In the peaceful green oasis of the garden, camellias flourish in stone urns and old-fashioned plants

View from the spiral staircase to the seating area. The carpet is the artist's own design for V'soke-Joyce.

OPPOSITE: The seating area, with Bedouin split-tapestry cushions and a collection of work by Irish artists.

The romantic Gothic-style back of the house looks out over a cottage garden.

The dining area. The table is dressed for Easter dinner, with a floor-length cloth and antique Irish crochet work. The ceramic bowl by Vivienne Foley is filled with traditional red-dyed eggs and camellias. In the background is a French Provincial chair.

OPPOSITE: *A collection of nineteenth-century jelly molds gives decorative impact to a corner near the seating area.*

grow beneath the clematis-hung cherry tree.

But any expectation of a cottage interior ends in surprise. One's initial impression is of light and space in a large open-plan room, two floors high in parts, running the full depth of the house. The focal point of the room is an almost sculptural pine staircase made from an ingenious French kit. And the eye is drawn up by its spiraling turns to a gallery with a matching balustrade specially crafted by a Cork joiner.

A rustic feeling is maintained in the plain wood floors and white-painted walls. Low-ceilinged areas of the room create more intimate spaces for dining and seating. Only the kitchen, bathroom, and bedroom are enclosed.

But the feeling throughout is of elegant simplicity. Interest is created by the interplay of varied spaces and by decorative details arranged with the sure hand of an artist who has worked out her own rules. One secret, that of getting away with eclecticism, is that quality must be the common denominator.

The seating area best illustrates this principle and the success of the cottage itself. A 1960s Form International chair sits happily beside a pair of French gilt wood chairs, and a day bed with Bedouin split-tapestry cushions. A collection of nineteenth-century jelly molds, paintings and drawings by Irish artists, and bark and branches gathered for a current project on trees intrigue the eye.

A still life on the kitchen bench, with a traditional wooden egg rack and starch jars holding flour and bread.

Still life in progress. The objects gathered for the study are laid out on a custom-designed ash table under the window, which was once the carriage-house door.

A Joycean Eyrie

Cityful passing away, other cityful coming, passing away too: other coming on, passing on. Houses lines of houses, streets, miles of pavements, piledup bricks, stones. Changing hands.

JAMES JOYCE, *ULYSSES*

It was near Merrion Square in 1904 that James Joyce arranged to meet his future wife, Nora Barnacle, on their first date, on June 16, a date later immortalized in *Ulysses* and now celebrated each year as Bloomsday.

The square was developed and laid out from 1762, following the establishment of the Wide Streets Commission in 1757, and was the first Dublin square to be planned as such, other squares having evolved in a more haphazard fashion. Unlike Parnell Square and St. Stephen's Green, Merrion Square has survived virtually intact, as a fine example of Georgian speculative development. The National Gallery is on the northwest corner of the square and above its portico is a luminous green room of the improbable shade that would result from the mixing of spring grass with bluest sky.

Its walls are virtually covered with gilt-framed eighteenth- and nineteenth-century oil paintings, and a large desk in the center of the room supports piles of papers. There is an agreeable hint in the air of the Bewley's coffee percolating in the corner.

Across the square past one of the tall brick terraces is another room in smoky delphinium blue, its walls similarly hung with groups of oil paintings. These two rooms encompass the life of Homan Potterton, director of Dublin's National Gallery of Art; his office and home are just a short stroll apart across the park in the center of Merrion Square.

His flat looks out over treetops of the square. And, true to Joyce's words, the house, once a grand town house like its fellows, has changed hands. The nameplates beside each doorway indicate the altered circumstances of fine residences, which now house flats or the offices of doctors and dentists.

Homan Potterton's drawing room is the essence of informal Irish style, which depends for its success on the happy arrangement of objects without any conscious attempt at design. Mr. Potterton cheerfully admits that his eyrie is an interior decorator's nightmare, a room that "just happened," where a scarlet sofa is cheek by jowl with yellow, turquoise, apricot, and green chairs and gold curtains hang against deep blue walls.

The city is blessed with green spaces. The view over Merrion Square and its central park.

The view over Merrion Square, framed in gold damask curtains.

Mr. Potterton doesn't accept the idea that pictures must be hung on pale, muted colors because the pictures themselves are colorful. He likes strong colors and uses them as boldly as possible.

The room is satisfyingly filled—nothing minimalist here—with favorite things. There is an opulent pile of cushions on the sofa, testimony to an earlier enthusiasm for needlepoint. A rare Irish gilt mirror featuring seahorses and shells, discovered in a junk shop, hangs over an eighteenth-century Irish mahogany side table; the walls are covered with groups of seventeenth- and eighteenth-century oils by French, English, and Irish painters.

Although he is an expert on seventeenth- and eighteenth-century paintings, Mr. Potterton is by no means a purist about what he collects. "I don't specialize in any way. I just buy things that I like."

The furniture and paintings have been acquired over the years, many of them during his tenure at the National Gallery in London. Not that there is any deliberate intention to collect, but when Homan passes an antique shop he naturally has to go in, and sometimes finds something he cannot resist. And so in the most natural and uncontrived way he has ended up with a room where the contents are a pleasant reflection of personal taste.

Irish gilt mirror, circa 1840, by the Delvecchio family hangs over an eighteenth-century Irish side table topped with Kilkenny marble.

OPPOSITE: *A collection of needlepoint cushions on the sofa. Above hang eighteenth-century Irish portraits by Robert Hunter and John Lewis. In the center is a seventeenth-century French oil painting of Artemesia drinking her husband's ashes.*

An Elegant Obsession

The afternoon mist had frozen away to nothing: their house, footlit by terrace lamps, ran its pilasters up into the glassy black night air.

ELIZABETH BOWEN, *THE DEATH OF THE HEART*

There is always between house and owner an observable relationship, ranging from mere marriages of convenience on the one hand to all-absorbing passions on the other.

Desiree Short's home is her grand passion, friend, and sometime provider. The house, she says, provides an ideal backdrop for her busy life, encouraging her to live up to its elegant standards. In return for love and restoration, the house provides home and workplace, and when times are hard it will gather itself for the effort and manage to generate extra revenue. Strongbow Productions recently commissioned it as a setting for the television serial "When Reason Sleeps."

For ten years Miss Short eyed the house from the windows of friends' houses across the street. They urged her to buy; she demurred. Then one night in the dead hour before dawn she woke to the certainty that she must buy it immediately. The contract was signed just

A view of Desiree Short's garden.

OPPOSITE: *The hallway, showing the huge fanlight of the exceptionally fine Georgian doorcase. The gilt mirror and console table are guarded by Italian terra-cotta busts of Diana and Apollo.*

A five-foot-tall Chinese palace vase makes a conversation piece for the drawing room.

a week before a rival buyer offered almost double what she had paid.

The house that she bought thirteen years ago is a twenty-two-room five-story house, built and adorned by the Dublin stuccodore Charles Thorpe in 1785. One of the finest houses in the street, it has what is arguably the finest Georgian doorframe in Dublin. Like an old aristocrat fallen on hard times, the house was down at the heels, yet retained all the features of its former grandeur.

The first priority in restoring the house was the basement. Rescued from damp and decay, this is now a large airy studio for Miss Short's china restoration business.

The first floor, the drawing room, and dining room have now been restored, the former with wainscoting marbleized by Paul and Janet Czainski in tones of the same gold as the Siena marble fireplace. The hall and staircase have been marbleized and ragged by another friend and annual visitor, the American designer Jim Rensch, who specializes in restoring mansions in his native Newport, Rhode Island.

In the absence of the considerable funds required to furnish the house in the original manner, Desiree Short's solution is to invest in eye-catching *objets d'art* rather than in much more costly period furniture.

The drawing room is the product of imagination and color. Pale gold walls offset a magnificent collection of blue-and-white porcelain from China, the Middle East, and Europe. "I know I have gone over the top," she says, "but having worked with porcelain for years I feel that I have earned the privilege."

An unfortunate aristocrat — Marie de Lamballe, close friend of Marie Antoinette, who was guillotined during the French Revolution.

An Irish gilt table from Limerick proudly carries a collection of blue-and-white Chinese vases of the Ming and Ch'ien Lung dynasties.

The fine Italian mirror reflects a seventh-century Tang horse and English chinoiserie figures. The Sienna marble mantel-piece encloses the unusual Irish steel grate.

In working on a house where she sees herself in the role of caretaker for future generations, Miss Short has tried to maintain the fine line between restoring and embellishing. She takes great care not to destroy or change the original character of the rooms but merely to enhance them.

This role of guardian is not without sacrifice. The house comes first; money that might otherwise be spent on holidays and other luxuries is swallowed up by the house's appetite not only for timber, plaster, and other basics but for finer things —porcelain chandeliers, paintings. But then, who would not make sacrifices for the companion of a lifetime?

Dublin Grandeur

Dublin, though a place much worse than London, is not so bad as Iceland.

SAMUEL JOHNSON, LETTER TO MRS. CHRISTOPHER SMART

It would be easy to suppose from the outside that number 13, Henrietta Street—a once-glorious street now bearing all the hallmarks of decline and neglect—is derelict. In fact, it is the home of Michael and Aileen Casey, who are mounting a remarkable operation to rescue a fine example of an early Georgian town house.

The impression of dereliction continues in the hallway, and passages show signs of demolition work. The room Michael Casey jokingly calls the ballroom is where his sons, Patrick (Casey maximus), Edward (Casey major), and James (Casey minor) play football. William (Casey minimus) is still too young to play. Only when a door opens on a reception room containing two green damask-covered swan-backed sofas does it become evident that the house is occupied.

Number 13 was built somewhere between 1720 and 1750 as a town house for Viscount Loftus, first earl of Ely. Designed on a palatial scale, with four stories over a basement, the house was subsequently sold to

Richard Pocock, Bishop of Meath. After the Act of Union in 1800, the fortunes of the houses in the city declined. The Irish Parliament was dissolved, and so town houses were no longer a necessity for gentlemen of rank. By the end of the nineteenth century, number 13 had become a slum tenement.

When Michael Casey bought the house fourteen years ago, with the assistance of the Georgian Society, there were eleven families, thirty-six souls altogether, in residence. The landlord reckoned there was room for one hundred tenants in all. The main floors had been divided to create further floors and the rooms, in turn, were subdivided by a rabbit warren of partitions.

These have now been removed, leaving behind a patchwork of color in the splendidly proportioned reception rooms, which, marvelously,

In the back drawing room hang three nineteenth-century portraits of as-yet-unidentified gentlemen. The marble is an eighteenth-century copy of a Roman bust.

A portrait of Anne Wadensford, later Countess Ormonde, copied in the mid-nineteenth century by Kirkpatrick from an original by the Irish artist Hamilton. The bust of the woman with the garlands in her hair is also from the nineteenth century.

still have their original details, moldings, paneled wainscoting, cornices, and architraves intact. And in a minimally furnished house, the fabric of the rooms and their original functions are laid bare.

When George I came to the throne in 1714 it was a time of relative peace and prosperity in Ireland. Dublin was growing in importance and by mid-century was to become the "second city" of Europe. For men of significance, a town house became an essential base from which to conduct business and wield influence. Their houses were not built with the comfort and convenience of the inhabitants in mind but rather to impress visitors with the splendor of the architecture.

That impression relied on the proportions of the rooms, on decorative plasterwork, on hand-blocked wallpaper and paneling, and on the splendor of the occupants' attire. Furniture at that period was still

OPPOSITE: *The portrait over the slab mantelpiece is of Josiah Hort, Archbishop of Armagh and Tuam. On the table below the portrait of the lady in blue is a collection of military helmets, including a shako that belonged to William Clements, third earl of Leitrim.*

On the drawing room chimney breast hangs a portrait of Constantine Phipps, first Earl of Mulgrave and Lord Lieutenant of Ireland in the reign of William IV.

extremely sparse and likely to be moved from room to room as the occasion suited.

As was the fashion of the period, the chief reception rooms were on the first floor, or *piano nobile*, away from the noise and smells of the street. And since there were a great many comings and goings by important callers, the hall and stairway were correspondingly grand. The impressive staircase at Number 13 occupies a two-story hallway with compartmented plasterwork and a first-floor gallery. It is cur-

rently being rebuilt by a Dublin joiner who is painstakingly reproducing every detail of eighteenth-century craftsmanship.

Michael Casey is a tremendous enthusiast of the eighteenth century. For him the house is not only a lifetime undertaking but a valuable source of discovery about the past. He explains the life style of the period in detail, producing with a flourish a miniature chamber pot from the cupboard behind the shutter to prove that the first-floor room overlooking the street was

Reference books and prints in the library.

Copied from a marble in Rome, this statue was part of a collection sent to George III by Pius VII. It arrived damaged, so the king never received it. The pedal car belonged to Michael Casey as a boy.

OPPOSITE: *A shabraque saddle cloth of the Fourteenth Hussars hangs over the end of the bed. A framed fragment of cloth from the throne of Marie-Louise (second wife of Napoleon I) hangs with a collection of military medals.*

used as a dining room. In a period when privacy was not much valued and the water closet had yet to be invented, the pot would have been used by both male and female diners.

The Caseys and their four young sons live in the house in much the same manner that the original occupants would have done. The only heating comes from turf or log fires, and furniture is minimal. The rooms contain a collection of portraits, classical statuary, and memorabilia, all of which is in some way connected with the house, the Casey ancestors, or the unfolding history of the city. Michael Casey knows the story behind every single item.

The restoration of the house is going ahead piecemeal, as time and a shoestring budget allow. All the original architectural details are being painstakingly put to rights before furniture, decoration, or, indeed, creature comforts can be considered. One finds oneself wishing that a fairy godmother might come to the aid of the Caseys, not with a magic wand but with a restoration fund.

The house provides a magnificent insight; in a strange and compelling way, the exposed, worn fabric of the house and the bare bones of its rooms speak far more evocatively of the past than any perfectly finished interior could do.

Memories from the Past

All the business of life is to find out what you don't know by what you do.

THE DUKE OF WELLINGTON

On the corner of the street where Handel's *Messiah* was performed publicly for the first time stands one of Dublin's oldest houses. There was a house on the site long before Handel's time, for the narrow road was one of the twelve original streets within the walled medieval city of Dublin. Maps of that time show a house occupying exactly the same site as the present building.

The house was built in the late seventeenth century in the Dutch manner and still retains angled chimney breasts (the walls in which chimneys are set) across the corner of the rooms. It was once a merchant's house; records show that in 1841 Thomas Holmes, an ancestor of the present occupants, was granted permission to run an "off-licence," or liquor store, in the ground-floor room, still referred to by the family as "the shop."

The house is four stories over a basement, brick faced and timber framed with an exposed beam running down the center of each ceiling. There is a single large room on each floor, with a tiny chamber behind each chimney piece. From the windows overlooking the River Liffey you can see a dozen church spires and the green dome of the Four Courts.

Today the house is an incredible living museum. Not only do the owners come from a long line of hoarders, they are also inveterate collectors with an innate sense of what will become interesting and valuable with the passage of time.

Every corner of the house has a particular theme, and not an inch of wall space goes to waste — even the stairwell is devoted to different military campaigns. In the red parlor on the second floor, for example, a bust of Pius IX presides over a collection of *Risorgimento* memorabilia, including sets of lead soldiers.

On the easel is an etching of a Victorian lady. The family still recalls lighting the Edwardian oil lamp.

A view of Dublin's Four Courts.

OVERLEAF: *A bust of Pius IX presides over the* Risorgimento *collection. The furniture includes a great-grandmother's velvet-covered suite.*

The furniture and bric-a-brac—including their great-grandmother's velvet-covered suite—has been handed down from generation to generation. Over the first-floor mantelpiece hangs a portrait of a great-grandfather who was killed on the Naas Road in 1864 when his horse bolted. The family still has a newspaper report of the fatal accident. Beside it hangs great-grandmother's black silk widow's jacket, still bearing the label of the Dawson Street maker.

Here, the past has not been lost. It is there in a host of reminders, from cannon balls from the Crimea, the Victorian dollhouse where grandfather kept his shaving things, to the picture of the great-grandmother, "who got married with five shillings."

The chiffonier, guarded by lithographs of French generals, a Royal Horse Artillery infantryman's mess jacket, and a trooper's tunic.

The angled chimney piece carries a portrait of a great-grandfather, killed in 1864. His widow's jacket hangs beside it.

LEFT: *A bust from the collection of Sir Oliver Lambart of Beauparc reflected in the mirror of a walnut Victorian chiffonier.*

OPPOSITE: *On the left is a bust by the Irish artist George Campbell. The washstand carries grandmother Esther Finlay's toilet set. The washbowl was used by succeeding generations to mix the plum pudding.*

By the Waterside

No matter where you go in Ireland, water makes its influence felt. It is there in that soft moisture-filtered light peculiar to Ireland. And it is there in the nature of the landscape and in the pattern of human settlement.

The Gulf Stream and the damp prevailing winds from the Atlantic are responsible for the greenness, for the subtropical plants that flourish in sheltered places, and for trees that grow faster than anywhere else in Europe. The mild climate and the year-round grass shaped the lives of a pastoral people and continue to do so.

Seaside buildings have differing characters very much dictated by their use. Color-washed fishermen's cottages are never far from the pier; sprawling Victorian villas in resort towns were built to house visitors or families on holiday. The round Martello towers—the most famous of which is Joyce's tower in Sandycove, immortalized in the opening chapter of *Ulysses*—were built around the coast as a defensive measure during the Napoleonic Wars. Coast Guard cottages were built on vantage points overlooking the sea, and castles and forts were often dramatically sited on high promontories to make them more impregnable.

The carriage house and staff cottages form a garage courtyard at the corner of the garden at Ely Lodge.

Of course, no one lives very far from the sea on an island that can be crossed in three hours' drive. But there are also over eight hundred major lakes and rivers in Ireland. It is rare to find a town or village in Ireland that does not have a river running through its heart or winding around its flanks. Often the river provided the very raison d'être for the place, offering deep water for a port, the power to drive mills, or the means to carry goods.

OPPOSITE: *The gardens of this house slope down toward the pinkish sands of Ballymastocker Bay.*

In the country, people have chosen to build near water for a great many reasons beyond the provision of one of life's necessities. The best land is often found in fertile river valleys, the rivers and lakes hold prized trout, salmon, and other fish. A view of peaceful water reflecting trees and sky offers a mystic calm, and rivers and lakesides were favorite locations for the "big houses" of the Anglo-Irish gentry. And if lakes were not already conveniently in situ, they were often created artificially to enhance landscaped gardens or parklands.

Perhaps the most romantic of all waterside dwellings are houses on islands. There is said to be an Irish island for every day of the year and that is without counting the many islands on lakes and rivers. Around one hundred of the coastal islands are inhabited and the majority are no more than five miles offshore.

The island communities often have deep-rooted folkways and traditions. On the remoter islands, such as Tory off the coast of Donegal where the painter Derek Hill helped found a primitive school of painting, the life style of the islanders remains relatively unaltered. On the Aran islands—Inishmore, Inishmaan, and Inisheer—Gaelic is still spoken. But today island populations are dwindling.

This cottage on the shores of Lough Swilly has been yellow-washed.

Other islands shelter romantic houses. The magnificent neoclassical Fota House on Fota Island, for example, is surrounded by an arboretum and houses a unique collection of eighteenth- and nineteenth-century Irish landscape paintings. It is no accident that some of the finest and most fascinating of the houses in Ireland are to be found by the waterside; the combination of land and water provides inspiration for painting, poetry, and architecture alike.

OPPOSITE: A collection of French Biot glass catches the light. The linen cloth is woven by McNutts of Donegal, and the Victorian chairs have been recovered in French fabric.

Reflecting an Artist

*The wrought-iron garden
chairs were designed
by Derek Hill and made
for him by a local
blacksmith.*

*The glazed foreshore and
    silhouetted log,*
*That rock where breakers shredded
    into rags,*
*The leggy birds stilted on their
    own legs,*
*Islands riding themselves out into
    the fog*

*And drive back home, still with
    nothing to say*
*Except that now you will uncode
    all landscapes*
*By this: things founded clean on
    their own shapes,*
*Water and ground in their
    extremity.*

SEAMUS HEANEY, "THE PENINSULA"

I t would be hard
to imagine two more different
worlds than the ephemeral business of stage design and the bare
survival offered by the rocky island
of Tory, off the coast of Donegal.
Yet the painter Derek Hill made
the transition from one to the other.

Derek Hill, apparently a man of
opposites—loving both sociability
and solitude, equally fascinated by
the decorative quality of Islamic
architecture and the starkness of
rock, sea, and sky—went on two
very different journeys in 1954.
One was a tour of Turkey with the
famous traveler Freya Stark, a trip
that fueled Hill's interest in Islamic
art. The other was to Ireland,
where he moved into St. Columb's,
a former rectory in the remote
parish of Gartan near Churchill,
County Donegal.

The move to Donegal was permanent and brought a new dimension
and strength to Hill's work as a
landscape painter. The scenery of
hills, lakes, and sea, with its con-
stant changes of light and weather,
was very different from the serene

*The view of the house
framed in beech trees
from across Lough
Gartan.*

*The studio at Gracie's
house in Churchill.*

*The gardens around the
former Glebe House, built
in 1820, were laid out by
Derek Hill with continued
help by James Russell,
who worked at Glenveigh.*

In the Reckett's-Blue hallway, a Chinese warrior wards off evil spirits and the vivid colors are picked up by a small Louis le Brocquy fruit still life. The mosaic-top table was bought locally.

landscapes of France and Italy where he had painted earlier.

Two years later he discovered the subject matter for his greatest landscapes on bleak, often storm-locked, Tory Island. He rented a hut there and one day, so the story goes, local man James Dixon watched him work and commented, "I could do as well." Hill gave him brushes and paints, other islanders followed suit, and the Tory Island Primitives were born. Derek Hill still returns to Tory to paint the rocks, cliffs, and ever-changing sea and sky.

His house at Churchill reflects Derek Hill's varied life and wide-ranging interests. He studied stage design in the 1930s in Munich and Paris, afterward traveling to Russia and the Far East. Later he worked in London and then in Rome as art

director for the British School. He wrote a number of books on Islamic architecture and is an inveterate collector of all kinds of decorative objects, from picture postcards to original William Morris designs. Wherever he went he brought back reminders of his travels—Turkish rugs, embroidery from Bukhara, Japanese prints.

His approach to interiors is both theatrical and highly decorative. The small entrance hallway, for instance, is a startling blue made from Reckett's Blue Bag (an old-fashioned laundry aid), and the hall archway is decorated with a design taken from Turkish window papers (used to keep passers-by from looking through the windows).

Much of the furniture in the house was bought in Donegal junk shops and warehouses, including his collection of bamboo furniture. The value of an object did not matter at all to the artist so long as it was pleasing; he collected cottage china—local Donegal spongeware and hand-painted rose-patterned Wemyss ware—long before it was fashionable to do so.

Although St. Columb's was remote, Derek Hill entertained many celebrities there, including the violinist Yehudi Menuhin, who sat for a portrait and joined in a *ceildh* (a party or gathering with music) in the kitchen. After his late neighbor *Inside the studio.*

The Italian marquetry-top table is paired with an English base and Regency-style chairs. The painting on the top right is by Sir Edwin Landseer, as are the other studies picked up by Hill.

Gracie's kitchen.

RIGHT: *The writing table is part of Derek Hill's collection of bamboo furniture.*

OPPOSITE: *Pale lilac walls are a foil for gold carpets and curtain in the drawing room. The Victorian chairs and footstool are covered with beadwork.*

OVERLEAF: *Derek Hill's bedroom. The iron bedstead is covered with embroidered Indian cloth, and the wallpaper was by Derek Hill's brother's firm, Green and Abbott.*

Henry McIlhenny sold his estate to the Irish government, Derek Hill decided to donate his Donegal home and three hundred paintings to the Irish nation. Now his house and possessions can be seen and enjoyed by everyone. Though he still comes to stay in the village of Churchill, where his longtime housekeeper Gracie has a cottage, Derek Hill now spends most of his time in Hampstead, London.

A Peaceful Legacy of Plantation

*I hear lake water lapping with
  low sounds by the shore;
While I stand on the roadway, or
  on the pavements gray,
I hear it in the deep heart's core.*

W. B. YEATS, "THE LAKE ISLE OF INNISFREE"

In common with the six counties of Northern Ireland, Donegal shares a long history of plantation. The long battle of Hugh O'Neill, earl of Tyrone, to rid Ulster of the English ended in defeat at Kinsale in 1603. Four years later, O'Neill and over ninety important Ulstermen went into the voluntary exile known as "the flight of the earls."

OPPOSITE: The ribbed vaulting over the staircase was painted to give a tentlike effect.

Looking from the big house down toward the ferry house and the still waters of Lough Swilly.

Plantation was seen as a means of subduing the troublesome province. Lands were confiscated, and settlers came from England and Scotland. The evidence of plantation is still there in forts, neat villages, and the way land is worked, for the planters favored arable farming, rather than the Gaelic pastoral ways.

Under the plantation scheme, the lands belonging to the manor of Killydonnell on the shores of Lough Swilly were granted to the English "servitor," Captain Basil Brooke. The remains of Brooke's plantation fortress can still be seen, though the lands were later leased to the Stewart family, who built the present house.

The exact date of the house is not known but it is thought to be about 1735, with the addition

The drawing room, painted to match the sea and sky. The mirror is one of a Georgian pair and in the foreground is an Irish hunting table.

of nineteenth-century "grandifications" in the form of plasterwork in the principal rooms and a pilastered porch.

The graceful three-story, seven-bay front with two small wings looks out across the lough to a peaceful patchwork of fields on the far shore. That the house was "bought for nothing" in the late 1960s is enough to make anyone eat their heart out. But the family who bought it found a house that had been empty for over twenty years. It had been used to store grain and was without light or plumbing. Miraculously, it was sound and the roof was still intact.

At first the family lived in the ferry house by the water's edge, using the windowless house only occasionally for parties. Later, a change in tax rates made it possible for the family to renovate, and they found that the house made them wonderfully welcome.

Black varnish was stripped from the floors, which were sanded and oiled with linseed, and hideous color schemes of brown and green were replaced with whites, cloud colors in the drawing room, and blues to match some magnificent William Morris curtains. The decor was devised by one of the daughters of the family who trained as an interior designer. The rib vaulting in the pretty Gothic Revival hall and stairway was painted scarlet and gray, creating a tented effect. And the walls of a maze of kitchens and pantries were knocked down to form a single room.

It is again a serene, sunlit house, facing southeast over the stretch of water where the ferry once carried produce from the peninsula en route to the city of Derry.

The master bedroom, with a family fourposter and a Victorian rocking horse rescued from some old stables.

Halcyon Days by the Lough

Now folds the lily all her sweetness up,
And slips into the bosom of the lake.

ALFRED, LORD TENNYSON, "NOW SLEEPS THE CRIMSON PETAL"

In a land of long histories and tall tales, few houses can have a stranger story than Ely Lodge. A home was built in 1830 on an island in lower Lough Erne, County Fermanagh, for the second marquess of Ely. It was partially built from the stones of Hume Castle, and was one of the first Palladian houses in Ireland designed by Richard Castle.

Extraordinary to relate, the house was blown up in 1870 to celebrate the coming of age of the fourth marquess and so that an even grander house might be built. If it seems a little hard to believe in such eccentric birthday behavior, there is the alternate theory that the house was destroyed to avoid having Queen Victoria to stay.

Neither Queen Victoria nor the new house ever materialized. The young Lord Ely spent his money instead on his other home, Loftus Hall in County Wexford, and all that remained of Ely Lodge was the stable block. This was purchased on his marriage by Lord Robert "Pud" Grosvenor, who made his home there. But when he succeeded as the fifth duke of Westminster, he made Eaton Hall in Cheshire his principal residence and used Ely Lodge as a holiday retreat. It is by no means a grand place, but a comfortable home where guests from all over the world were entertained at shooting and yachting parties.

The building provides a pleasant series of long low rooms, no more

A view of Ely Lodge across reed-fringed Lough Erne.

OPPOSITE: *The flagstones from the former stables were used to create a terrace, where flowers fill stone horse troughs and flour troughs from a flour mill.*

This thatched retreat was used as a guest house and was a favorite spot for picnics and barbecues.

The study is dominated by Benjamin West's 1728 painting of William of Orange at the Battle of the Boyne. The log carrier was specially made for the late duke of Westminster.

than a stall wide. The late duke added a new wing and portico and incorporated some features from the old Eaton Hall, which was demolished to make way for a new building. The conservatory was added in 1980 by Dowager Duchess Viola, who adopted Ely Lodge as her permanent home. The flagstones that floored the stables have been used to create a terrace overlooking the gardens and Lough Erne, where the family and guests would gather in good weather.

The house reflects the dowager's choice of warm colors, golds and pinks, a perfect foil for the cool colors of water and grass outside. The house is quite simply furnished with a combination of auction finds, family pieces, and masses of fresh flowers from the garden. Tragically, the dowager was killed in a car accident in 1987. The house has been left to the family land agent, bringing another chapter in the story of Ely Lodge to a close.

In the drawing room, a mahogany wine cooler is used as a jardiniere. The Steinway grand piano belonged to the Dowager Duchess Viola, an accomplished concert pianist. The Victorian prie-dieu chair is from the family chapel.

The drawing room is a warm golden corn color. Among the paintings are landscapes by Donegal artist Derek Hill and a small Constable, as well as a Poussin, Millet, and a Dutch landscape by Molenaer.

The late duke's bedroom. Percy French watercolors and a sketch of the duke's labrador hang over the Windsor chairs.

The tiles in the downstairs cloakroom, from the old Eaton Hall, are decorated with the Grosvenor G and portcullis from the family's armorial bearings. The late duke's silver-backed hairbrushes are kept polished to perfection.

OPPOSITE: *The flower room at Ely Lodge.*

Island Estate

The first chapter in the history of Fota House is set in the early eighteenth century, when John Smith Barry, fourth earl of Barrymore, built a hunting lodge on Fota Island in Cork Harbour, part of large Cork estates granted to his ancestors in 1179.

Subsequently a great deal of the family fortune was squandered by the seventh earl of Barrymore. Three of his children were members of the notoriously fast Carlton House set, the drinking and gambling companions of the Prince Regent. Much can be inferred from the prince's nicknames for them, which he based on the medieval gates of London: The eighth earl was known as "Hellgate"; his brother, who had a club foot, was called "Cripplegate"; and his sister, who had a colorful turn of phrase, "Billingsgate," after the market where sharp-tongued fishwives plied their trade.

OPPOSITE AND RIGHT: The gardens in the arboretum at Fota showing a rare Cryptomeria japonicas spiralis—said to be the tallest in the world—and plantings of pampas grass, water lilies, and gunnera in the lagoon garden.

In the 1820s John Smith Barrymore, known as "John the Magnificent," decided to enlarge the existing house and make it his principal home. He commissioned the architect Sir Richard Morrison to carry out the alterations and—a rare feature—to design estate build-

In the rear elevation of the house, the original plaster finish, designed to throw the carved stonework into relief, has been stripped off and left bare.

Detail of the section of the restored ceiling, with frescoes painted by Ian Cairney and gilding by Susan Mulhall. Before the restoration, the drawing room was used to store lawnmowers and ping-pong tables.

ings, including a huntsman's lodge, which is a scaled-down version of the house.

Morrison's design, which turned the original square house into an H shape, included the most important room in the house—a magnificent neoclassical hallway with graceful Ionic columns in yellow *scagliola*—and added an imposing dining room with a screen and gray marble Corinthian columns, a Doric porch, and a graceful staircase lit by a tripartite window incorporating a floating dome. The famous arboretum, housing rare subtropical trees grown in the shelter of timber belts, was created by John's son, James.

Years passed, and in the 1970s the last of the Smith Barry descendants left Fota. In 1975 the island estate was purchased by University College Cork with a view to using

OPPOSITE: *The drawing room, with a custom-designed carpet and 1880 painted ceiling and gilt fixtures by Sibthorpe and Company, the Dublin firm of decorators. Through the doorway is the anteroom, which acts both as a prelude to the drawing room and an introduction to Richard Wood's collection of paintings.*

the land for dairy science training. Coincidentally, local businessman and art collector Richard Wood was searching for a place to display his unique collection of Irish landscape paintings for public view.

A most unusual deal was struck, in which the house was leased to Mr. Wood, he restored and furnished the interiors, and his eighteenth- and nineteenth-century paintings were put on view, not in a soulless gallery but in the far more appropriate setting of a great home.

The interior restoration was supervised by architect John O'Connell, in close collaboration with Richard Wood. The result is a series of charming rooms that have none of the dead air of a museum. There are no red ropes or "do not touch" signs. Instead, it seems that someone has only just vacated the library

Victorian landscape paintings hang over the chimney piece of the watercolor room. The yellow walls have been dragged, and the urns are miniature versions of the Morrison designs.

chair, abandoning the books scattered on the table by the turf fire. You expect at any moment to hear the rattle of silver as the butler supervises the setting of the great dining table.

And indeed the table is laid frequently. It is part of Richard Wood's philosophy that the house, having outlived its original purpose, should find a new one. And so the rooms of Fota are used for concerts, dinners, fashion shows, and other events by appreciative residents of Cork, which perhaps explains the happy, lived-in feel about the place. Empty jeroboams of champagne on the dining-room sideboard and fresh flowers in all the rooms add to this atmosphere.

The restoration of the house was a labor of love and enthusiasm that took seven years, but it has by no means been overdone. Most of the plasterwork has been left in the original white aged to gray, which shows the detail far better than any pristine emulsion. The rooms are underfurnished, like any home in the making.

The hall is still painted in the original green, and the only additions were a collection of marble busts and two copies of the classical urns from Lyons House, County Kildare, which look as though they were made for the niches at either end of the imposing room.

OPPOSITE: *One of the glories of Fota, Morrison's neoclassical tripartite hall with columns of gold scagliola. Morrison's copies of the urns at Lyons House, County Kildare, look as though they were made for the niches. The skirting and pedestals were marbleized.*

The central section of the drawing-room ceiling had collapsed and had to be restored. One of the challenges was to recreate the original look of the rooms, restoring or copying as closely as possible such period details as wallpaper and curtains. Another task was finding appropriate furnishings. The curtains in particular are a triumph, the ones in the dining room having been copied from an 1841 sketch by Anna Maria La Touche of the drawing-room curtains at Bellevue; in the library, valances and poles were rescued from Ballingall House and curtains made specially to match.

The pictures form a subplot of their own. When Richard Wood began collecting, fired with enthusiasm by art historian Anne Crookshank, little was known about Irish landscapes. His collection, which recaptures a lost portion of Irish heritage, is arranged chronologically with a room devoted to each distinctive development of style, giving a fascinating insight into how closely Irish thinking mirrored European ideas of the period. The paintings reflect classicism, the Age of Reason, the Romantic period, Victorian subject paintings and, in the twentieth century, open-air painting typified by the work of Mildred Butler and her studies of country houses.

The library walls are hung with topographical paintings belonging to the Age of Reason, in contrast to the Augustan Age or idealized landscapes of the drawing room. The crimson wallpaper by Coles is a close replica of the Edwardian original.

OPPOSITE: The unusual combination of gray fireplace and green wallpaper is linked by the gray cornice and pale green ceiling. An Empire-style bed is covered with Irish linen and the painting is a Victorian subject study.

Richard Wood frequently shows visitors around himself, giving amusing and detailed commentaries on his treasures and the restoration work. One of his stories concerns the provincial eccentricities of an Irish gilded side table in the anteroom. The claw feet stand on balls like circus performers, the correct form for carving the backs of the claws having clearly been a mystery to the craftsman, who carved horses' fetlocks instead. The lion's mask on the front of the table has been given a wonderful drunken leer. It is the kind of story that makes people look at every detail of their surroundings with a new appreciation, which, says Richard Wood, is exactly what Fota is meant to be all about.

In its most recent chapter, the story of Fota has taken an unhappy turn. Some board members of the University College Cork voted to sell part of the estate to a developer. Part of their proposed plan would involve the building of more than three hundred time-share holiday homes, in a complex of Italian-style flats overlooking the gardens immediately behind the house; the plan also involves destroying the shelter belt of trees around the island, which could cause great harm to the arboretum. The agreement would also require the developers to decorate the interior every five years, without necessarily consulting or

The wallpaper in the Shamrock room dates back to the 1870s. Underneath the George I carved gilt mirror is an inlaid Killarney jewelry box.

working with Mr. Wood. Such an arrangement hardly seems compatible with the preservation of rare hand-painted wallpaper and painted ceilings.

If the plan goes ahead, Richard Wood will pull out of Fota, removing his paintings and antiques, and the interiors as you see them here will be lost. The fate of Fota currently hangs in the balance.

Detail of the Irish linen spread, with shamrock embroidery and needlepoint lace.

The principal bedroom, hung with rare hand-painted paper rescued from Killeen Castle. The bed is an eighteenth-century Irish fourposter, the mirror is Queen Anne, and the cradle was presented to the mayor of Cork in the last century.

OVERLEAF: *The anteroom. A David Roberts landscape painting of the Powerscourt Estate, which demonstrates Lord Powerscourt's management of his lands, hangs between two of the seventeenth-century Flemish works that strongly influenced Irish painters. The statuette is of George IV in the robes of a knight of St. Patrick and leaning on the harp of Ireland. The chairs are copies of originals at the nearby house of Dunkathel.*

OPPOSITE: *A bathroom with a collection of prints depicting Castle Freake and the Freake family.*

The cool octagonal game larder with a chandelier of game hooks beneath a central vent.

The dressing room of the principal bedroom, with mahogany-cased bath.

Living in the Country

There are several striking things about the Irish countryside. One is that houses are scattered widely apart. Rather than being clustered around the nucleus of a village or town, many buildings are quite isolated, set at some distance from the road.

Irish history is responsible for a pattern of development very different from the village-related settlement in England and Europe. Scattered dwellings are part of a very ancient system in which a pastoral people tended to settle in the middle of their land. Plantations reinforced this pattern, especially in the South and East of Ireland, where landlords held huge tracts of land and the farms and houses of tenants tended to be dotted around these holdings.

Another characteristic feature is the number of abandoned cottages and farms, particularly in the remoter areas of the country. Before the Great Famine, the population of Ireland was over 8 million. After three years, the potato blight and disease took their toll among a people largely dependent on the potato as their staple diet; the population dropped by 2 million. A million had died and a million had emigrated.

The decline in population continued, as rack-renting landlords evicted pauper tenants, laying the foundation for the future "land wars." Farmers could no longer risk dividing already small holdings and so a pattern ensued of late marriage for sons who would inherit. Other members of the family saw no future in Ireland and emigrated. Significant migrations to the towns and cities also depopulated the countryside. The popu-

OPPOSITE: *A brocade screen shelters a family of ceramic swans.*

lation of Ireland, North and South, is today still only around 5 million, and the impact of history can still be seen clearly in the countryside.

Another striking aspect of rural dwellings is the way that houses appear either to be mansions or cottages, with very little in between. And to a great extent rural homes can be divided into houses—from the very grand to the modest—belonging to the landlord class and the cottages and small farms of the tenants.

The gulf between big house and cottage marks to a great extent the division between the peasant population of Ireland and the Anglo-Normans and later the planters who replaced the Irish lords and chieftains. The high estate walls and stands of timber that surround ascendancy houses are a marked feature of the countryside.

The cottages and small farmhouses of rural Ireland were traditionally built of local material. Thatched mud cabins were still common among poorer tenants until after the famine. Bricks were a rarity, with most cottages being built of local stone. Walls would be rendered, then white- or color-washed, and the roofs were made of slate or different types of thatch, reed, oat, or rush, depending on what was available.

Building styles tended to vary by region. The older cottages and farms had a pleasing harmony between the design of houses and their settings. The choice of site, the use of local materials, and a natural instinct for the appropriateness of a house to its location all made for a happy marriage of house and landscape.

A romantic gateway to a country house.

Sadly, this is not the case with newer constructions. The appearance of the ubiquitous bungalow, built with total lack of sensitivity to surroundings and without reference to tradition, is one of the visual blights on an otherwise unspoiled countryside.

OPPOSITE: *In the older section of the Berkeley Forest, a pine dresser holds blue-and-white china.*

The Donegal Dollhouse

Once upon a time there was a very beautiful doll's-house; it was red brick with white windows, and it had real muslin curtains and a front door and a chimney.

BEATRIX POTTER, *THE TALE OF TWO BAD MICE*

There is a curious house in Donegal that had its top story missing. It belongs to two sisters, one of whom likes to look after outdoor things, the garden and animals; the other sister likes to sew and collect toys.

The house is divided in two halves, one for each sister, so that each has a separate territory as well as different responsibilities. The staircase leading to the first floor up the low-beamed hallway splits in two at a landing, making the demarcation of territories easier.

A great many dolls also live in the house, and among a large collection of toys are three dollhouses. One is a grand Georgian house, a reminder of the time when such houses were designed as builders' models rather than playthings. Another fact makes this story sound even more like a Beatrix Potter tale: there is a cat called Tabitha Twitchit (Tablets for short) who also lives in the house and is inclined to make inroads on the cheese biscuits when no one is looking.

The history of the sisters' house is vague, and like many Irish houses it has a wing that dates from an earlier period. But there is a legend attached to the place—which might or might not be true. The property was once owned by a Catholic who was married to a Protestant woman, at the time when the Penal Laws were in force and Catholics were not allowed to own land. This woman invited a Protestant vicar's wife to tea. Having fallen in love with the house, the vicar's lady informed on the couple, causing a forced sale and acquiring the house herself in a most unchristian manner. The ousted wife departed, leaving a curse on the place.

The supplanting rector subsequently built a smart new house nearby around 1820. The earlier

The Edwardian drawing room showing the original beams, with the unusual feature of a window over the fireplace.

OPPOSITE: *The Georgian-style dollhouse, from Dublin. The doll is Victorian with wax features and real hair.*

The dollhouse kitchen, complete with plate covers hanging over the range and hen cage—in which the hen waited its fate—by the dresser.

house became a steward's residence, and the second floor was removed by the vicar, no doubt to keep the steward from getting ideas above his station. Both houses were bought by the present owner's grandparents but the new house subsequently burned to the ground; perhaps wondering at the efficacy of curses, the family moved back to the original house. Their descendants live there to this day.

The story of the Georgian-style dollhouse is better documented. It had belonged to some Dublin cousins and eventually came to Donegal as part of a growing collection of toys. Over the years it has been splendidly refurnished. With Tablets around, there are no bad mice to create havoc in the miniature rooms.

The more important members of the doll family carry in their pockets "papers" with information about their backgrounds. They are quite an assorted family, including an 1880 Quaker lady with leather

The elegant dolls' drawing room. The carpets were specially made for the house and the whatnot is filled with miniature knickknacks.

limbs, dressed by a relative, a Mrs. Booth Clibborn, a saucy 1930s boudoir doll with a very made-up face, and a sad case who was washed up on the beach and had to have her leg replaced.

The dolls live a sheltered existence in the upstairs rooms, cosseted, mended, and given new gowns and underclothes at need. In return they are an endless source of entertainment, not only for their owner but for visitors large and small.

And the moral of the story is, I suppose, that one is never too old to play with dolls.

The nursery in the doll-house, with washstand, china wash set, a nurse doll, and an inch-long china baby doll.

OPPOSITE: *Part of the doll family: left, a Quaker doll; seated, a 1930s boudoir doll with a painted face; and standing on the bed an Edwardian doll—a Miss Bewley—and an early Victorian doll who has a new gown made by her owner.*

Tales of the Unexpected

. . . nature so mild and benign and proportioned to the human constitution.

BISHOP BERKELEY, *SIRIS*

At Berkeley Forest, the presence of three generations of Irish dwellings offers a perspective on the way Irish landowners have lived through the centuries.

In the grounds are the remains of a tower or stronghouse, a reminder of Ireland's turbulent past. The homes of plantation or Anglo-Norman families and also those of Celtic chieftains had to be defensible until the sixteenth, even into the seventeenth, centuries. The three- or four-story towers were designed more for security than for comfort.

As times became settled and prosperity increased, a small gentleman's residence was built looking across the gently rolling land to the distant Blackstairs Mountains. This building was incorporated as a wing of the late eighteenth-century house built by a Colonel Deane to reflect the grandeur of his station in life as a member of parliament and relative by marriage of Bishop Berkeley, for whom the house is named.

Set in parkland, with Suffolk Cross sheep lying under the shade of beech trees, the low ochre-washed house with its pillared portico seems at first glance typical of the medium-size Irish country house. Inside, however, Berkeley Forest has many unexpected features.

Where you might expect a dining room somber with vast mahogany sideboards and the requisite hunting table and dining chairs, there is an all-white room, its floor stenciled with a blue-and-white geometric design painted by Lily Butler. In place of the usual rent table and hunting trophies in the flagged hallway, there are Austrian pieces in carved oak, Victorian toys, a child's wicker phaeton, and an early perambulator made by a local carriage maker. In a bedroom where faded

The glow of the hallway beyond the porticoed pillars welcomes visitors.

Berkeley Forest—set in parkland grazed by a flock of Suffolk Cross sheep.

BELOW LEFT: *In the green bedroom, toile curtains and bedspread are stenciled with crown and Celtic motifs. Beside the bed is a wooden shrine.*

BELOW: *A chaise lounge and white-painted wicker furniture make a romantic corner in the peacock-blue bedroom.*

A Victorian rocking horse and phaeton from the collection of antique toys.

chintzes and floral papers would be the norm, there are instead brilliant emerald walls with white toile curtains and a bedspread stenciled with green crowns and Celtic motifs.

It seems that unusual influences are at work, and indeed they are, for Berkeley Forest is the home of a Danish count and his wife, Irish artist and designer Anne Griffin.

Over the years the house had suffered a decline in fortunes, as have so many Irish houses, and had been let to a succession of tenants. It took twenty years for the present owners to get the house in basic order, to banish the black varnish from the floors and restore the agreeable air of serenity that characterizes the place.

Unless they come with an accretion of inherited family furniture, such houses are difficult and impossibly expensive to furnish in the original manner. Anne's solution was to use decorative devices to please the eye; her criterion for furniture is simply that the pieces should work well together.

The most fascinating room in the house is the upstairs saloon, now home to Anne's collection of period costumes and antique dolls and toys. In the afterglow of sunset silent figures stand, a ghostly feminine gathering from the past, in crinolines, bustles, and the satin-panniered gowns of the mid-eighteenth century.

The costumes bring home how tiny our ancestors were. Anne had to create ingenious figures of wire and padding to fit diminutive waists and slender wrists.

The same ingenuity is evident elsewhere in the house. In a teenage daughter's room the walls have been stenciled with a striking tulip design. The bed boasts a quilt decorated with ruched and appliquéd chintz flowers of Anne's making. In the main bedroom the walls are an exotic peacock blue; gauzy drapes hang à la polonaise over the bed, hiding an infrared lamp that conquers the damp of Irish winters.

Every house has its own particular feel to it. At Berkeley Forest the various elements of the family's busy lives—farming, collecting, painting, and other absorbing interests—flow together agreeably under the roof of a much-loved home.

In the teenage daughter's room, the stenciled tulips and appliqué quilt are Anne Griffin's handiwork.

OVERLEAF: *A family portrait in progress, after Gainsborough, in Anne Griffin's studio.*

Through the Looking Glass

I had your letter by the last post,
and before you can send me another
I shall set out for Ireland. . . .
I think, since I have known you,
I have drawn an old house upon
my head.

JONATHAN SWIFT, LETTER TO VANESSA

The plasterwork is a reconstruction of a Robert West ceiling. The chairs and sofa are Louis XVI and the chandelier is Waterford.

Lit by magnificent Regency candelabras and a Waterford chandelier, the dining room is all white.

Candlelight gleams on a collection of glassware.

The meandering driveway builds up a sense of anticipation that is eventually fulfilled by the house hidden round its mysterious bends.

You come upon the house suddenly —behind a belt of sheltering trees. The first intimation that this is a place as full of the unexpected as Alice's dream world beyond the looking glass is a pink ribbon fluttering frivolously from the granite portico. A massively ancient lime tree and two giant Florence Court yews suggest a centuries-old history.

No one knows the exact provenance of the house. The age of the trees on the estate suggests that it is Queen Anne (1702–1714). For such a relatively modest house it has very grand details — magnificent doorframes surrounding original mahogany doors, an imposing staircase, and two beautifully proportioned reception rooms, which take up the entire ground floor.

OPPOSITE: *The granite portico was rescued from a derelict house. A trio of hens strut the gravel forecourt.*

Claus Michel and his wife, Iris, found the house twelve years ago, and it took six months of building work before the place was habitable. "All we had was the roof," says Iris Michel. "The floors had to be dug out to a depth of two feet and French drains dug around the house. It was like a Roman excavation." The windows and floors had to be replaced, the walls treated for damp. Inside was a decorator's nightmare. There were layers of flock wallpaper; the bannisters had been painted gold and the stairwell mauve.

The nightmare has now been banished. In its place are ethereal dazzling white rooms where daylight or candlelight is reflected in mirrors and glassware. In the drawing room the seating is draped in ghostly white duckcloth, and in the dining room, white-painted wicker chairs from Poland surround the glass table. Even the carpets and

OPPOSITE: *Tinna Park, guarded by an Irish yew and framed in the branches of a chestnut tree.*

The classical plaque is a copy and the dining room chairs are white-painted cane.

floors are snowy, their pristine whiteness protected by practical runners that can be laundered. The only concession to color in either room is gilt and greenery.

The most remarkable achievement of all is the graceful plasterwork of the ceilings and the classical plaques adorning the walls. The ceiling by Robert West, the leading stuccodore of the mid-eighteenth century, was rescued from a now-demolished house in Parnell Square, a dramatic operation that involved sawing the stuccowork in sections, reassembling and restoring it on the floor of a barn at Tinna Park, then casting a replica of it to provide a ceiling for the drawing room. The centerpiece of the original was missing but the central boss was ingeniously copied from another West ceiling in St. Stephen's Green; this particular section of plasterwork was sawed out and used as a mold before it was replaced.

Today, no one would ever guess that the delicate garlands of leaves and flowers were not the original. Like most enthusiastic restorers, Claus and Iris have lots of stories about their home. The granite portico, for instance, was acquired from a derelict house in exchange for a bottle of perfume—admittedly a very large bottle of perfume. The marble fireplace in the dining room is also a refugee, salvaged from Powerscourt and still bearing burn marks from the fire that tragically gutted the great mansion in the early 1970s.

Iris believes in subtracting from rather than adding to furnishings. "Normally houses of this type are furnished in period style," she says. "I find that boring or too heavy."

OPPOSITE: *The doorways of the dining room and drawing room are arranged enfilade.*

A copy of a Stapleton plaque over the Adam-style fireplace. The gilt wreath and the gold-rimmed glasses are eighteenth-century pieces.

Eloquent Interiors

They buried him, but all through the night of mourning, in the lighted windows, his books arranged three by three kept watch like angels with outspread wings and seemed, for him who was no more, the symbol of his resurrection.

MARCEL PROUST, *LA PRISONIERRE*

Prospect House is aptly named. Where you might least expect it in the flat land of County Kildare, the house offers an enchanting view drawn straight from an eighteenth-century landscape painting. Horses graze in peaceful parkland and a dramatic cloud-filled sky hangs over a distant view of the Dublin mountains.

Granite steps lead up to fanlit front door.

The front of the house perfectly fits the ideal of a modest Georgian gen-

The stairs were painted a simple black, and the classic reliefs of urns designed by Timothy.

tleman's residence. A steep flight of granite steps climbs to the fanlit front door; old-fashioned roses grow against the area railings.

Inside the house can be sensed an eloquent unseen presence, inexplicable, even haunting, until its source is known . . .

An invitation to participate in ROSC, Ireland's quadrennial contemporary art exhibition, brought Timothy and Isabelle Hennessey to Ireland in 1980. They stayed on, living in a flat in the Palladian splendor of Castletown House, beguiled by the poetic nature of Irish landscape, fascinated by large country houses.

Like many Irish houses, Prospect was situated to make the most of the view of the surrounding landscape. Once owned by the earl of Milltown, it is a very typical five-bay, two-story-over-basement, mid-eighteenth-century house with

charm but no particular architectural merit. In its heyday the estate was a self-contained world with farm buildings, dairy, stables, and walled garden.

When the present owners found it, the house was in very poor repair. Now it has been restored simply, painted white throughout and floored with dramatic black-and-white tiles. The house reflects their views on art—that classic architecture is very much related to literature.

There are many examples, both seen and unseen, of Timothy's theory regarding literature. Urns hold butterfly-shaped pieces of text from James Joyce's *Ulysses*, from *Finnegan's Wake*, and from Proust. He believes that words have a separate existence in space and time, a life of their own. Accordingly, each room has a different text under the

The new terrace. Here, Timothy's decorative cypress trees are echoed by the trees in the parkland.

The bedroom bookshelves are filled with Isabelle's work. Over the bed is a painting by Irish artist Phillippa Garner of an interior at Castletown House. The cushions are Fortuny.

floor: Yeats in the library, Proust and Joyce in the drawing room, Plutarch in the morning room, and Aristotle in the kitchen. Hence the unseen presences.

The most dramatic aspect of the house is the black-and-white treatment of the hall and stairway. Classical plaques with urns and geometric paneling have been used to create a sense of the Renaissance, emphasized by Timothy's cypress trees, part of a former exhibition featuring a formal garden.

The library is Isabelle and Timothy's favorite room. It is colored in rich Renaissance shades with a collection of Fortuny cushions, cut-velvet Fortuny curtains, and a collection of French Art Nouveau vases filled with fuschia, iris, and lilies. In particular, the library reflects their idea that rooms, too, are works of art, to be arranged as paintings are composed. Their furniture is a combination of family pieces, flea-market finds, and auction bargains. Such finds are more of an adventure, Isabelle thinks, because they free you to transform them.

Isabelle worked for a number of years with the Parisian designer Marcel Rochas, designing foulards and silks. Her studio is filled with current work, which evokes an Irish garden, executed in leaves and petals.

Isabelle's work, based on rose petals and leaves from an Irish country garden.

The basements of Irish houses are often sadly neglected, but at Prospect House the lower floor comprises a dining room of grand proportions, an airy white kitchen, and guest rooms.

In the quiet of the cobbled stables at Prospect hangs one of Timothy's collages. It is a lament for four thousand great Irish houses that have been lost, demolished, burnt, or allowed to fall derelict beyond redemption. A sad litany.

The 1950s bathroom mirrors were auction finds.

OVERLEAF: *Prospect is a typical mid-eighteenth-century house with a five-bay front. The household was a self-contained world with its own dairy stables and farm.*

Few, if any, see great houses as works of art but rather as manifestations of ascendancy rule, believes Timothy. "Castletown is the Acropolis of Ireland, yet no one sees it that way . . . It is a kind of Em-

peror's clothes in reverse."

The great houses of Ireland are rich reflections of unrecognized social and artistic expressions. Perhaps it is as Proust wrote: "The true paradises are the paradises we have lost."

OPPOSITE: *A French bookcase, used to store fabrics, takes pride of place in the morning room. The flower engravings are family treasures.*

The Big House

In Ireland, the idea of the "big house" evokes rich imagery: high estate walls, long bumpy drives, hunt terriers racing out of an open front door, worn granite steps, gleaming rumps of ancestral mahogany, that faint smell of damp and woodsmoke, windows that look out over timbered parkland.

The "big house" is a universal Irish expression, actually a euphemism for "landowner's home." The big houses may have been big in relation to tenants' homes, but the term may cover anything from vast palaces to modest mansions.

Ireland has a quite extraordinary number of large houses that were built in the eighteenth and nineteenth centuries. *Burke's Guide to Irish Country Houses* alone lists two thousand, and there are thousands more. They are largely, though not exclusively, the legacy of a history of invasion and colonization that created a new landlord class.

OPPOSITE: *At Castletown Cox, a sixteenth-century Italian cherub stands, holding a shield bearing the Medici coat of arms, on the acrylic table designed by Baron de Breffny. Beyond are views of the lake created by the Archbishop and the dome and campanile of the East wing.*

Before 1603 and the defeat of Hugh O'Neill, earl of Tyrone, at Mellifont most of the land in Ireland was owned by Catholics, either the Celtic Irish or the "Old English," the Anglo-Normans. By 1660 ownership had effectively changed hands, largely through confiscation, plantation, and the ruthless policies of Oliver Cromwell, who declared that the Irish could "go to Hell or Connaught." A new Protestant landlord class was created and its ascendancy endorsed by the later Penal Laws against Catholics.

The great majority of large houses were built over a period of little more than a century. Before 1690 unfortified houses were virtually unknown, but as times became more settled land-owners abandoned their "tower houses" and began to build more comfortable homes.

Very few of the earlier houses, usually modest manors, remain. They were either knocked down to make way for grander houses or altered, often incorporated into fashionable "improvements." Many older houses were used as back wings or "tails" for later houses, as at Berkeley Forest. Prehen House, Derry (illustrated here), is a fairly rare intact example of an early eighteenth-century house.

Building in Ireland broadly followed the architectural fashions of England, but styles often became somewhat changed in the process of crossing the Irish sea. These idiosyncrasies are part of the charm of Irish architecture. Fashions arrived later here and changed more slowly, so that it is quite common to see a house of one period with details that are a hangover from an earlier date.

The less-wealthy gentry frequently designed their houses without benefit of an architect, or "artificer," and their builders either copied ideas from other houses or used the pattern books that became available mid-century, which sometimes resulted in delightful eccentricities in design.

The great Irish houses are not so large, cumbersome, or pompous in design as their British counterparts. And the successive fashions in architecture, such as Palladianism and neoclassicism, were often adapted or watered down to suit Irish taste, climate, and pockets, creating a distinctive and pleasing Irish style.

Two of the most influential architects of the first half of the eighteenth century were Sir Edward Lovett Pearce, who introduced the Palladian style to Ireland, and his pupil, Richard Castle. The great houses, like Castletown Cox (featured here),

Castletown, Russborough, and Carton, in which the central block of each house was flanked by pavilions, are wonderful examples of the Palladian style.

More common, and uniquely Irish, are the "tall houses" of the period. Three or four stories high, they are nearly as high as they are wide, and almost like Georgianized versions of their forerunner, the tower house.

The building of elegant mansions was very much an expression of status; the rank and privilege of a gentleman derived from his ownership of land. And the building of a fine estate house, surrounded by landscaped parkland and embellished with the work of fine craftsmen, was a way to demonstrate wealth, taste, and refinement.

As the English gentry set the pace, the Anglo-Irish attempted to follow suit, often without sufficient funds. The great irony about many big houses is that their owners were often living beyond their means—certainly beyond the means of their miserable tenants. Families were frequently ruined by building activities or subsequently never had the money to live in the grand manner for which their homes were designed.

The decline and fade of former gentility is a striking aspect of the Irish big house. Seldom is there money to renovate or replace original interiors.

One of the great glories of these interiors is the work of Irish craftsmen, particularly the stuccodores. The Italian Francini brothers popularized elaborate Baroque plasterwork featuring high-relief figures, fruit, flowers, and trophies, which provided an inspiration for Irish craftsmen. Fashions in plasterwork then progressed through the lighter, more fanciful, Rococo, of which Robert West was a leading proponent, to the delicate neoclassical style, which used Roman motifs. Michael Stapleton's work provides some of the loveliest examples of this style. The pro-

At Ballyorney House, the beautifully restored Baroque ceiling from O'Connell Street carries festoons and swags of naturalistic fruit and flowers. The drawing room is conceived like an art gallery—painted poppy red and hung, three-deep, with a collection of eighteenth-century paintings.

gression of plasterwork fashions in Ireland can be seen in Ballyorney House.

The second half of the eighteenth century saw a gradual shift to neoclassical and Gothic or romantic styles in the bigger houses. Richard Morrison's neoclassical designs for Fota House and Charleville Forest by Francis Johnston, a fine example of a nineteenth-century Gothic castle, are both featured here. Very typical of Irish style are the numerous modest-size houses in the "late Georgian" style that continued throughout both William IV's and Victoria's reign.

The spate of building tapered off after the Famine, was revived briefly in the late Victorian era, and virtually ended with the agricultural depression of the 1880s. The Wyndam Act of 1903, which allowed the Senate to purchase the lands of estates and sell them off to tenants, set the seal on the declining fortunes of the ascendancy class.

Some big houses were burned during "the Troubles" in the 1920s, though not nearly so many as are popularly supposed. Far more houses have become derelict or have been "tumbled" during the intervening years by local farmers interested only in the land, not the prohibitively expensive large houses.

Attitudes toward the big houses have changed gradually from the antipathy and bad feeling that followed the Famine to apathy toward their fate. Now there are the glimmerings of awareness that the big houses are part of the Irish heritage, often containing fine examples of work by Irish craftsmen, and that the houses and furnishings are works of art that can all too easily be lost.

A Palazzo in Arcadian Fields

Here every view, hill vale and grove,
With various wonders grac'd
The noble owner's judgement prove,
His genius and his taste.

SAMUEL WHYTE

In the mid-eighteenth century, when Michael Cox, Archbishop of Cashel, decided that he must have a home to reflect the importance of his station, he rode his lands repeatedly with his architect, Davis Ducart, in search of the most perfect setting.

Both the choice of site and of architect proved to be inspired, for the Italian Daviso de Arcort (whose name was Irishized to Ducart) built Ireland's loveliest Palladian villa in the rolling meadows above the Suir Valley. Castletown Cox was completed in 1771. The silhouette of the Archbishop's palazzo, with its flanking pavilions surmounted by distinctive domes, is echoed in the rounded peaks and plateaus of Slievnamon and the distant Comeragh Mountains.

Perhaps the ecclesiastical connection brought divine protection, for Ducart's graceful design in dressed sandstone and unpolished Kilkenny marble and the splendid plasterwork by local stuccodore Patrick

Castletown Cox.

Osborne are intact. The house has escaped the hand of later Georgian and Victorian "improvers" or the fate of repeated lettings suffered by so many Irish houses. Castletown Cox has had only three changes of ownership since it was built, and the intermediate owners merely installed electricity and made minor alterations.

Certainly in its choice—if houses can be said to choose—of present owners the house is blessed. For when after many months Baron and Baroness de Breffny finally succumbed to Castletown's extraordinary spell, the house became the property of a couple who are not only enthusiastic collectors but who also view themselves as the guardians of a precious heritage.

When the Baron and Baroness de Breffny married, they had between

OPPOSITE: *The box garden was laid out about 1910 by Lady Eva Wyndham-Quin.*

them four homes: they decided to make a fresh start by disposing of them all and putting all their eggs in one basket. They were also searching for a challenging project to work on together; in Castletown, they found an all-absorbing life's work.

Now, ten years later, the Archbishop's palazzo is a glowing tribute to the attention that has been lavished upon it. Moreover, the house has about it that air of supreme contentment found in those who are not only loved but understood.

One of the Breffny's priorities was to ensure that all the pictures, furniture, and decoration were in keeping with the eighteenth-century character of the house. They have also tried to ensure that nothing should detract from its original design or from the splendor of Osborne's plasterwork.

In the entrance and staircase halls, the detail of each festoon and swag ornamenting the meticulously carved ceilings and panels is thrown into sharper relief by the use of palest grays and off-whites. The plasterwork looks as freshly minted as the day in 1774 when Patrick Osborne presented his bill for £696, 10 shillings, and 5 pence for the embellishment of the main rooms. The walls in the ground-floor reception rooms have been ragged or stippled and the wainscoting in the corridor marbleized.

The compartmental box garden, once filled with bedding-out plants in the days when there were twenty-four gardeners at Castletown Cox, now treated by Baron de Breffny with gravel over an underlay of polyethylene.

Decorative blue-and-white Spanish plates with hen egg cups on the Irish country dresser.

OPPOSITE: *A needlework sampler of Hibernia weeping, a copy of Thomas Moore's* Songs of Old Ireland *and a Belleek figure of Hibernia.*

The house is now used very much as it would have been in the time of the Lord Archbishop. In keeping with a period when the main impact of rooms was created by the grandeur of their proportions and splendor of their plasterwork, the great entrance hall has been left virtually empty. The Archbishop's drawing room, saloon, and dining room are furnished with period pieces and the walls are hung with portraits and landscapes.

The original breakfast parlor has been rescued from an ignominious fate as a kitchen, and is now the library. And the basement, once abandoned to the rats, is now restored to its former use, complete with flower room, laundry, wine cellars, and staff sitting room. The original kitchen, where a copper *batterie de cuisine* gleams on the walls, is now the breakfast room.

But the main bedroom, still known as the Archbishop's bedroom, belongs completely to the present. It is a breathtaking place filled with light and whiteness. Glass and acrylic furniture add to the room's translucence, and the only color comes from three treasured Ben Nicholson oils.

There is always some new project underway in a house that is still evolving. Beside the east wing, work is in progress on a new knot garden, which will be planted with herbs.

Yet although the restoration and embellishment of the Archbishop's palazzo is an ongoing labor of love, it is by no means unrequited love, for on those occasions when the guest rooms are full and a company of up to sixteen gathers in the candlelit dining room, then, says Baron de Breffny, you can positively feel the house responding.

The gleaming copper batterie de cuisine *from Vienna, bearing the Hapsburg crown.*

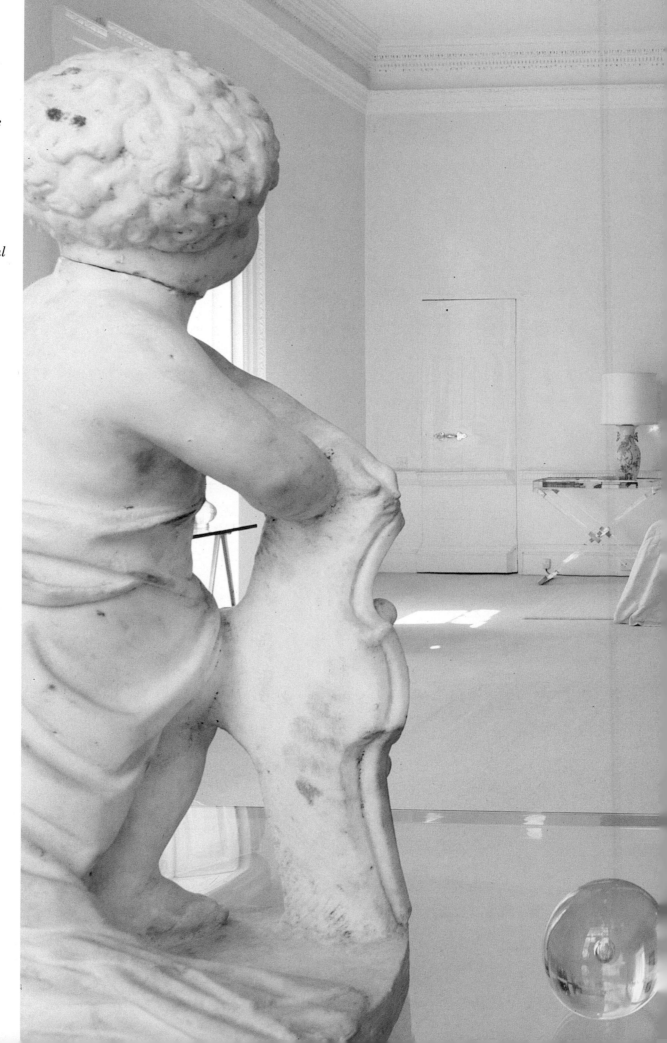

The Archbishop's bedroom, on the same grand scale as the drawing room immediately below. The painting is by Patrick Scott. On the cantilevered Italian table stands an architectural toy by David Hicks.

In the entrance hall hangs a portrait by Stephen Slaughter of Anne O'Brien, wife of Archbishop Cox, who died in childbirth, leaving his lordship inconsolable. The cartouche was specially designed as a surround for the painting. The eighteenth-century busts are of two Roman emperors.

A Georgian Heritage

See grandeur here by social virtue grac'd
The Manor noble, as refin'd the Taste.

HENRY JONES

The great Portland stone fireplace in the hallway of Newbridge House bears the coats of arms of the Cobbe family, who built the house and owned it for two hundred and fifty years. On the armorial shield are two swans ambulant with the motto *Moriens Cano* ("Dying I sing").

The motto is singularly appropriate in the case of Newbridge House. Generally when changed times and circumstances force families to sell grand old houses, the contents are auctioned and scattered and yet another small chapter of history is torn asunder.

The swan song of the Cobbes ends on an altogether happier note, for the house, contents, and demesne were sold to Dublin County Council. The furniture, paintings, and possessions built up over two hundred fifty years and the intimate insight they provide into the past are there for all to see.

The descendants of the Cobbes, far from being dead, still come to stay in the house. On special occasions they light the candelabra and dine in splendor in the Rococo dining room and, in so doing, give their ancestral home that indefinable lived-in feeling so lacking in other houses open to the public.

The house reflects a family history of upward social mobility. In 1717 the Reverend Charles Cobbe came to Ireland as humble chaplain to his cousin, then a lord lieutenant. By 1732 he had risen rapidly through the ecclesiastic ranks to become the Bishop of Kildare, and was

OPPOSITE AND LEFT: The gallery was used to display classic statuary brought back from various Grand Tours, and was a prelude to the grandeur of the red drawing room.

The front elevation of Newbridge has changed little since it was built two-and-a-half centuries ago.

Part of the magnificent collection of paintings purchased by Thomas Cobbe, displayed in the red drawing room. To the left is an Oriental carp jar.

then made Archbishop of Dublin in 1746. In 1837 he had Newbridge built, probably by Richard Castle, to reflect the grandeur of his position.

The original house was a relatively modest classic rectangular building. It proved, however, not quite impressive enough for the fashionable wife of the Archbishop's heir. The sister of the marquess of Waterford, Lady Elizabeth Beresford brought money into the family and added a large wing to the back of the house in about 1760. And there Lady Betty entertained lavishly in the red drawing room, a suitable setting for her husband's collection of seventeenth- and eighteenth-century paintings, which he acquired with the advice of the Reverend Matthew Pilkington, the Vicar of Donabate and author of *The Gentleman's and Connoisseur's Dictionary of Painters*, the first reference book on paintings.

OPPOSITE: *The white marble fireplace in the red drawing room.*

The room is a veritable showcase for the work of Irish craftsmen of the period. The elaborate plasterwork is attributed to Dublin stuccodore Richard Williams. The harp, still complete with instructions for playing, came from Egans of Dublin, and many of the contemporary pieces of furniture came from the Dublin firm of McWilliams and Gibson and Robinson. The crimson damask wallcovering, coordinating curtains, and carpet date back one hundred and seventy years.

The house provides an interesting insight into changing tastes in decor. The plasterwork in what was originally the drawing room (and, with the later additions to the house, became the library) has a delightful Baroque ceiling depicting the four seasons, a theme typical of the early Georgian period. The plasterwork in the dining room, executed about twenty-five years

A pier glass in the red drawing room hangs over a companion eagle console table. Both are late Georgian, made by Irish craftsmen.

The marble fireplace in the entrance hall features the Cobbe coat of arms with swans ambulant.

The dining room at Newbridge. Beside the black marble fireplace is one of a pair of Chippendale tables, part of the original furniture of the room. The dining chairs are nineteenth-century Irish variants in the Chippendale style.

later, shows the progression to the later Rococo style.

While the earlier rooms are paneled and painted in the fashion of the period, the red drawing room reflects the more lavish later Georgian style. Wallpaper was introduced around the middle of the century, first imported from China. The early hangings were hand-blocked and made in four-foot squares. Carpets became common only after the middle of the century.

One of the high points for visitors to Newbridge is the "Museum of Curiosities." Started by a far-sighted member of the Cobbe family in around 1790, the room, with its specially designed showcases and chinoiserie panels, houses weird and wonderful objects brought back by family members from their exploits around the globe. No doubt there were fascinating stories attached to the objects, which range from an Indian dagger to an ostrich egg laid in Dundalk in 1756. The museum is thought to be unique in Ireland and Britain.

One of the display cabinets in the "Museum of Curiosities," created around 1790. This unique room was used to display items family members brought back from their adventures abroad.

The library desk—a copy of a French eighteenth-century bureau plat.

The front of the stone house. The quoins are of ashlar stone and the Greek Revival pediment was added around 1760.

In the salon on the piano nobile, the papier-mâché gilt furniture from India was part of a suite from the red drawing room in Castletown. On top of the cabinet are pieces of costume jewelry said to be from a Diaghilev ballet. The painting is a seventeenth-century landscape after Claude.

A View Over History

*I came on a great house in the
middle of the night,
Its open lighted doorway and its
windows all alight.*

W. B. YEATS, "THE CURSE OF CROMWELL"

It was Lady Peck, born Winifred Knox, who first suggested the restoration of Prehen, a Knox house, to her daughter-in-law (the mother of the present owner). And in 1971, at the height of "the Troubles," the house near bomb-torn Derry was bought by Lady Peck's granddaughter, Mrs. Peck, in order to save it.

The rescue operation was just in time, for the roof was leaking, pigeons were roosting in the bedrooms, the dining room was being used to store coal, and the house was on the verge of becoming a victim of its own extraordinary history.

Parts of the house date back to 1640 and from its vantage point high on the east bank of the Foyle overlooking Derry City, the house must have looked down on many a scene of strife. It is thought that during the Siege of Derry in 1689, in which the Protestant Apprentice Boys locked the gates of the city against the forces of James II, the Catholic pretender, some of his more irregular followers ripped out the paneling of Prehen House for firewood.

It is rare to find a house of this early period intact, untouched by rebuilding and relatively unscathed by history.

With architectural advice from the Hon. Mariga Guinness, Jeremy Williams, and Ada Leask, the family began to restore the house, removing sixteen partitions that divided the original rooms, taking out Victorian grates, replacing missing chimney pieces, and remodeling a corner of the boudoir ceiling that had fallen down.

Rare painted strapwork was discovered under the grime on the halls and boudoir ceilings, and classical medallions were painted in the entrance hall by Alec Cobbe (of the Cobbe family of Newbridge mentioned elsewhere in this book). The large hall is very typical of this period; flagged and virtually unfurnished, it was intended to impress.

Additions in keeping with the period of the house include black and white marble flags in the dining room and handsome bookcases in the library—these were ingeniously embellished with carved and gilded corbels from the now-ruined Eyrecourt Castle, County Galway, as well as with acanthus leaves from the frieze at Delville, Dublin.

Mrs. Peck has used strong Georgian colors in some rooms, often copying the shades used in such great houses as Carton and Castletown, with a Chinese blue for the saloon, Roman red in the dining room, peacock blue for the Empire-style bedroom and a strong golden yellow for the staircase hall. The library, which would originally have been paneled in a dark timber, is brown. The rooms with strapwork have been kept white—not dead white, but a distressed finish that looks far more appropriate than pristine paint would.

The house provides a perfect setting for a magnificent collection of furniture built up over the years, many pieces of which were acquired from the sales of the contents of some of the great houses of Ireland. Some of the rooms in Prehen House have been given particular themes: there is one bedroom with Empire-style furniture and another bedroom featuring a collection of Dutch marquetry pieces.

There is a story attached to every possession, and pieces are often the subject of intriguing speculation by the Pecks. What, for example, is the mysterious domed mansion that appears in the background of a painting of an Irish boy dressed as a Roman emperor? Was George Knox, whose miniature hangs in the music room, really a rebel in 1798 or was Evelyn Waugh right when he suggested in his *Life of Monsignor Ronald Knox* that he was an agent provocateur? Theirs is an exploration of the past that is fascinating and full of discovery. One can see why the Pecks are never, never bored.

OPPOSITE: *A corner of the library, with an eighteenth-century needlework chair. The table—one of a pair—was brought by Mrs. Peck's mother from New Orleans.*

The former day nursery, now a snuff-colored gentleman's bedroom with a magnificent collection of Dutch marquetry pieces.

The classical hallway with its strapwork restored. The medallions were painted by Alec Cobbe, and the bust on the right is of Antinous. The twin heads are "the Man of Thought" and "the Man of Action," Seneca and Brutus, respectively.

The dining room has been flagged in black and white marble. The frescoes were painted by Mrs. Peck for a Roman party. A fifteenth-century Cordoba leather screen hides a trompe l'oeil fresco. The mahogany sideboard and dining chairs are Irish.

A Venetian mirror hangs in the skies of a series of murals by Mrs. Peck. This one depicts the Bay of Naples and a castle after David's painting The Rape of the Sabines.

The stairway, with a painting of George III by Alan Ramsay.

Victorian Splendors

Coming up the avenue in the February dusk he could see the flash and shimmer of firelight through the naked windows of the library. There was something unearthly in those squares of pulsing light that fretted the shadowy facade.

ELIZABETH BOWEN, "THE NEW HOUSE"

BELOW: *A view of the grounds from the roof and the house seen from the pike lake, and the formal Italian garden.*

The south-facing windows of Temple House frame a silver sheet of lake and the imposing ruins of a castle, built by the Knights Templar in A.D. 1200, that gives the place its name. As in so many Irish houses, the site has a history of occupation stretching back through centuries.

When Alexander Perceval, known as "the Chinaman," received plans by post for the enlargement of Temple House, County Sligo, he wrote back, saying the projected building was "not large enough."

Today the house remains much as "the Chinaman" planned and furnished it in 1863, at a cost of three quarters of a million pounds. It is an example of the luxurious Victorian style made possible by an imported fortune founded on trade.

Incredible as it may seem, most of the building of Temple House was directed from abroad, for Alexander Perceval was based in Hong Kong working for the Oriental trade company Jardine Mathieson. Trade with the Orient made him extremely wealthy, enabling him to buy back the family estate that had been sold after the Famine to an evicting landlord whose name is still reviled in the area.

Following the typical pattern of Irish building, a new wing and servants' quarters were added to the original 1820 Perceval home, resulting in a house with ninety rooms, thirty-nine of them in the basement alone. Much of the furniture bought for

OPPOSITE: *The vestibule and white sandstone staircase, lined with family portraits arranged above the original specially designed carpet.*

OVERLEAF: *The formal gardens, which were laid out beside the lake in the Italian style in 1864.*

the house at that time was designed for the principal rooms by the Bond Street firm of Johnstone and Jeannes. As was usual, the kitchen gardens, the imposing stable yard, and the walled kitchen gardens were sited some distance away from the house.

Alexander Perceval's fortune also enabled him to reinstate tenants who had been scattered as far afield as the United States and England and to have new estate cottages built —a benign action rare in those post-famine days. On his return to Ireland bonfires were lit on every hill between Carrick on Shannon and Ballymote. But the celebrations were short-lived, for two years after his return "the Chinaman" died, leaving a widow and five children.

The Percevals, an old Norman family related by marriage to Strongbow's cousin, came to live in Temple House in 1665, and an Alexander Perceval still lives at Temple House today, farming four hundred sixty acres of a thousand-acre estate. Times have changed. Before the First World War there were eleven women and five men working in the house and five men and seven boys working in the gardens. Now Mrs. Perceval copes with the help of Kathleen, who has worked for the family for three generations, and one or two au pair girls.

Boots for every occasion, from fishing to shearing, lined up by the hall stand.

But—barring the absence of servants—little has changed. Visitors (the family accepts paying guests) find the interiors in Temple House frozen in the amber of time, preserved by the decline of family fortunes to that state of faded gentility so evocative of the grander kind of Irish style.

Electricity wasn't installed at Temple House until 1957. Splendid original plumbing, including a Shank's Patent Compactum Compendium water closet is still in situ. But aside from a few concessions to modernity, such as an alternative heating system—the original was capable of burning one-and-a-half tons of timber a day—the furniture and furnishings remain in untouched Victorian splendor, complete with curiosities brought back by "the Chinaman" from the Far East. There is a cavernous hall

featuring a mosaic floor, cases of stuffed birds, enormous pike from the lake, game trophies, and a large assortment of boots.

The vestibule has an imposing white sandstone staircase and landing with pilasters and wrought-iron bannisters; it is used to display a collection of family portraits. The drawing room and dining room demonstrate the sheer enthusiasm of Victorians for filling their rooms to capacity with newly mass-produced furniture. The drawing room seems faintly ghostly; dust covers protect once-green damask silk upholstery, faded now to the color of ivory.

In the bedrooms visitors can sleep in the half-tester beds with matching suites of furniture. The carpets and hangings are the originals, and guests are asked not to pull the curtains that time has made fragile but to use the shutters instead.

It is a small price to pay for living in the style to which Alexander "the Chinaman" had become accustomed.

OPPOSITE: Trophy heads and cases of stuffed birds and fish by Williams, the Dublin taxidermist, line the entrance hall.

*The drawing room, with
the original hangings,
rug, pelmets, and match-
ing mirror all designed for
the house in the 1860s.*

The entire suite of dining-room furniture was made to match by the London firm of Johnstone and Jeannes.

An Architectural Perspective

. . . the distinguished part of men,
With compass, pencil, sword or pen,
Should in life's visit leave their
name,
In characters which may proclaim
That they with ardour strove to raise,
At once their arts and country's
praise
And in their working took great care,
That all was full and round and fair.

MATTHEW PRIOR, "PROTEGENES AND APELLES"

The 1810 fanlit doorway of Ballyorney House.

Usually the history of an Irish house can be traced from the date of the building, through later embellishments and changing taste in furniture and decor.

At Ballyorney House the pattern is reversed, for beyond the frontage of an early nineteenth-century house time steps backward architecturally. Possibly the dower house for the great Palladian mansion of Charleville, Ballyorney was given a new front wing in 1810.

When the present owners moved there fifteen years ago, it was a typical small Georgian country house with stables at the rear. Now it has become the house of two interesting architectural tours de force: one traces the architectural forms of

Irish domestic building back to the Middle Ages, whereas the other follows the history of Irish plasterwork and interior design from early Baroque to the later Rococo.

To the earlier back wing of Ballyorney has been added a Gothic-style tower complete with a spiral stone staircase and Gothic windows rescued from a deconsecrated church and from a building in Hume Street, Dublin. It was designed by the architect Jeremy Williams, who has worked in collaboration with the owners on all the additions to the house.

Architectural history has been taken a further step into the past. Hidden behind the house is a room designed to fulfill the same functions as the banqueting halls that were once a feature of medieval chieftains' castles. Built within walled courtyards, only one or two of these buildings survive today.

Seen from the garden door of this hall, the pointed peak of the Sugar Loaf Mountain presents a dramatic view framed between florence court yews. The classic doorway, salvaged from a doomed building, is a suitable preparation for the drama within. The high coved roof was specially built to house a Rococo ceiling rescued from Grove House in Milltown, Dublin.

The classic Georgian front of Ballyorney House was added to an earlier building.

The eau de Nile *dining room, hung with portraits and landscapes from an eighteenth-century collection. The Rococo ceiling was rescued from a threatened house in Dublin's Dawson Street. The fireplace is early nineteenth century, ornamented with classical motifs.*

In what is known locally as "the ceiling that couldn't be done," the swirls and curls of stuccowork are being reassembled in place partly from the original and partly from molds taken from the original to replace the damaged sections. Supporting the design are four magnificent Corinthian columns from a church at Borrisokane that is now used as a factory.

At the front of the house a dark narrow hallway was removed so that one now steps into a large room, painted a sunflower yellow. The bow window of this room forms the axis of the L-shaped series of main reception rooms. In each direction an enfilade effect—which was a feature of grand eighteenth-century houses—has been created with new doorways.

Here, the architectural "refugees" have been used to splendid effect to demonstrate the development of Irish plasterwork, from Baroque to neoclassical. The rooms have been devised like art galleries, painted in strong colors and triple hung with a collection of eighteenth-century paintings. The earliest ceiling—appropriately used in the earliest part of the house—came from Templeogue House, Dublin, and the plasterwork features one of the four winds in the central boss. Busts of the Domville family of Santry Court dating from 1740 pre-

side. The paneling and woodwork date to the same 1730s period as the ceiling.

Perhaps the most fascinating ceiling of all is the one in the drawing room. It was reproduced from a surviving quarter of the Gilbey ceiling in O'Connell Street, which had been rescued and stored in an office in Mountjoy Square before being vandalized. The design is an example of Baroque at its height—the ceiling positively drips with cupids, larger-than-life flowers, and exotic fruits, including bananas. The ceiling was completed by taking casts from the original.

Ballyorney provides an intriguing insight into the evolution of Irish architecture and interior design. It is also an architectural home of rest, for the treasures it contains would not otherwise have survived to give visual pleasure.

The rooms, framed in Carolinian doorcases salvaged from a Wexford house, have been arranged enfilade.

OPPOSITE: *Sunlight streams into the unfinished banqueting hall.*

A grand piano fills the embrasure of the hall bow window.

The finial in the Gothic-style stairway designed by Jeremy Williams is surmounted by a guardian angel.

The crimson study was built to complete the enfilade arrangement of the rooms. Chinoiserie-style cabinets have been built into the alcoves and the carved gilt mirror is Irish.

Hideways and Retreats

Ireland is full of secret places. A turn off any road becomes an unexpected voyage of discovery. In a country where the scenery changes constantly, especially in the West and on the coasts, you can never tell what is around the next corner.

The next bend in the road could reveal a ruined medieval tower, or a sandy cove guarded by cliffs, or a still lake populated only by fish and wildfowl. It might unveil a deserted stone cottage waiting to be reclaimed or a small Georgian house surrounded by trees. Exploration off the beaten track almost invariably leads to the discovery of secret, beautiful places.

In a sense, many of the houses featured in this book could be described as hideaways. Their remoteness, or the way they are hidden behind timber and high demesne walls or down little-frequented lanes, makes each a kind of retreat.

A knowledge of secret places and of the lie of the land has been a necessary part of the folklore of Ireland at times, making it easier to lose or defeat an enemy by using pathways known only to the trustworthy across treacherous bogs. It is still possible to get lost in the countryside just half an hour's drive from Dublin, wandering a maze of winding small roads or walking in the splendor of the Wicklow Mountains.

This is a country where you can find peace and quiet, and be alone if you want to. With fewer people in the entire country than there are in the world's major cities, the roads are comparatively empty. Ireland is the most sparsely populated country in Europe. There are around five and a half million people in

OPPOSITE: Steppingstones across the Stuarts' water garden. In the distance, the shoulders of the Wicklow Mountains.

A patchwork of fields claimed from the windswept promontory surrounds the Ungerers' cottages.

Ireland, North and South, whereas Britain has a population of fifty-five million.

There is no shortage of buildings hidden away in unexpected places or in remote spots that make the most perfect retreats. The combination of seclusion, peace, and wonderful scenery has made Ireland a chosen sanctuary for many. From the monastic seclusion of their hillside, the Stuarts can look over the peaceful valleys and hills around Laragh in a place that is hard to find, yet is just an hour's drive from Dublin.

Families like the Walkers spend years searching for the perfect spot to base their holiday home; the Walkers eventually found theirs in a remote corner of County Cork. And you couldn't have

View of Ballinterry from over the fields. The back of the house was originally slate-clad; two of the seven blocked windows on the top right were uncovered after two hundred years.

a more dramatic setting than the home of Tomi Ungerer—a whitewashed cluster of cottages on a clifftop swept bare by the Atlantic winds. This is one of the rewards of Ireland, being able to find your own ideal retreat.

Irish people tend to think of Ireland as a place they leave. From the "flight of the earls" in the seventeenth century to the "silence exile and cunning" of James Joyce and to the tens of thousands of young people who are emigrating today, Ireland is the place they have left behind.

But for others Ireland remains a place of retreat, a sportsman's paradise and a haven from the pressures of twentieth-century living.

Mountain Peace

Beyond, beyond the mountain line,
The greystone and the boulder
Beyond the growth of dark green
*   pine,*
That crowns its western shoulder,
There lies that fairy land of mine,
Unseen of a beholder.

FANNY ALEXANDER, "DREAMS"

The Stuarts' house is a totally unexpected sight on the slopes of Paddock Hill, above Laragh, County Wicklow. The track winds between twisted thorn bushes and rowan trees, culminating at a low group of stone buildings that look as though they belong high in the foothills of the Himalayas.

There are more surprises to follow. Passing through a wicket gate and up steps through a series of terraces, visitors enter the house through a thick forest of tropical plants, reaching luxuriantly toward the glass roof of a conservatory. The living areas are on one side of this exotic vestibule, the main bedrooms on the other. Beyond the huge kitchen with a high skylit roof,

The house is approached through a series of garden terraces. In the center is the conservatory entrance that joins the living and sleeping areas of the house.

pillared steps lead up to the drawing room with a view over the pine-clad ridges of Brockagh (Badger) Hill.

The other side holds the bathrooms, the children's bedroom, a study, and the main bedroom with timber-clad dormer windows and a balcony looking out over the valley. The Stuarts, who frequently travel in the Far East, wanted to create a house with a monastic feel about it. They based the plan for their home on the existing layout of shepherd's cottage and outer buildings, and the house, built without architect or plans, evolved in phases. Ian Stuart, who is a sculptor, did much of the stonework.

The site and layout of the house have much in common with a traditional cottage. The building faces south, tucked into the sheltered side of the hill, and true to tradition, the main part of the house is one room deep and the building runs east-west.

In the past, stone or timber from former dwellings were often recycled and incorporated in a new building and the Stuarts' house is no exception. The King posts, a key feature of the design, came from a derelict poorhouse and are used to support the roof.

The house is full of exotic objects brought back from the Stuarts' travels—Indian and Thai statues,

a collection of bonsai trees from Thailand, shells picked up from Caribbean beaches, Kerala jewelry boxes from Rajasthan, exotic fabrics and rugs.

The furniture is an eclectic mix, including limed oak tables bought from the sale at Coolatin House, cane pieces from the Netherlands, wickerwork chairs from England, and local pine dressers.

Outside, a series of garden terraces are sheltered on three sides by the wings of the house. Graduated steps and walls in granite have a sculptural quality; nearby Ian has created a water garden with steppingstones and standing stones.

A strange peace prevails.

The steps leading from kitchen, with its recycled King posts, to drawing room are guarded by palms.

Corke Lodge

There was a rich trim air about the house. The rooms inside would be warm and full of flowers. There would be very delicious tea.

M. J. FARRELL (MOLLY KEANE), *THE RISING TIDE*

Corke Lodge was built as a retreat for Georgina McGann, the jilted daughter of a well-to-do Anglo-Irish family. Her unworn wedding dress is still at the former family home at 77 St. Stephen's Green, its virginal folds now guarded by Loretto nuns.

But no spinsterish spirit of disappointment lingers in the 1840 Lodge. Rather, the house has about it the air of a holiday villa, with an almost Mediterranean feeling suggested by the surrounding cork and evergreen oaks reminiscent of olive trees—Miss McGann subsequently found solace with a more reliable suitor.

When architect and designer Alfred Cochrane took possession of Corke Lodge in 1979, he decided to enhance this feeling and play up the villa aspect of the house, which is just a stone's throw from the sea on the outskirts of the Victorian resort town of Bray. He also made a feature of the duality of the architecture. Corke Lodge has a classical front and a Gothic-style back incorporating part of an older house. Such "two-faced" houses are not uncommon in Ireland; these features are a symptom of changing tastes in architectural styles. Alfred elaborated on the themes, continuing the classical motifs in the front rooms and giving those at the rear Gothic-style details.

The drawing room, for instance, was transformed to give the impression of a Mediterranean loggia, the walls painted with trompe l'oeil frescoes of Alfred's birthplace, Beirut. A great jardiniere filled with palm trees and brilliant Egyptian striped fabric add to the exotic mood. The walls are hung with architectural prints collected by Alfred when he was a student in Rome, and the room has been brightened with the addition of Gothic-style sandstone windows salvaged from the demolition of Glendalough House.

This dragon chair is from the Alfrank line.

The bathroom is enlivened by political prints and features a Victorian washstand and the original claw-foot bath.

OPPOSITE: *Architectural prints collected during Alfred Cochrane's student days in Rome hang on the chimney breast.*

The matching Gothic arches of Glendalough's porte-cochere have been used to create a cloister beyond the adjoining room. Further exotic illusion is added to the vista with a hammock slung among real and painted greenery.

The ground floor is given unity by a cool blue-and-green color theme and, in contrast, the colors upstairs are warm and earthy. Another of Alfred's architectural windfalls — he found the ornate screens and paneling from a church in the trash — have been ingeniously used to design a Gothic-style library on the first floor. A series of recesses exaggerate the room's size and house, variously, a day bed, books, stairs to the master bedroom, and a bar, creating a self-contained lair for Alfred.

Corke Lodge and its estate were acquired in 1905 by Alfred's great-uncle, Sir Stanley Cochrane, who owned the adjacent grand but landless Woodbrooke House. It served as a stewards' house and later as a temporary home to such glamorous tenants as Katharine Hepburn and Geraldine Fitzgerald, while they were on location at the nearby Ardmore film studios.

Faced with a house much in need of decoration and some structural repairs, Alfred Cochrane took the opportunity to make changes where major work was needed. The stairs

had to be replaced, but instead of using the original stairwell Alfred built a totally new flight of stairs, in the postModern manner. In the dramatic blue marbled and mirrored inner hallway, the steps are set between ramps, and their relocation has allowed the opening of a vista — through the hallway and out the back entrance — of a distant Gothic Revival folly.

In the dining room the architectural feeling has been enhanced by marbling the architraves and skirting in the same gray-green as the mantelpiece. Instead of conventional mahogany, a glass table resting on columns adds to the feeling of space in the all-white room.

The ground floor is a setting for Alfred's Alfrank line of furniture designs. Executed in glass and steel or painted wood these postModern

OPPOSITE: The cast-iron radiator becomes part of a decorative theme, with an arrangement of dried wheat, a carved sconce, and a chaise lounge covered with striped mattress ticking.

The library. The Gothic-style paneling came from a deconsecrated church; the turkey rug provides the strawberry color scheme.

designs forge an all-important link with the past by using mythological themes.

Our sensible ancestors built high beds to avoid the drafts created by bedroom fireplaces. Alfred took this idea further by mounting his bed on a stepped dais that doubles as storage space. The medieval tented theme of the terra-cotta master bedroom is created by ornate brass rods—a flea-market find—

The main bedroom. The bed is raised on a dais; the hangings and quilt appliquéd with Alfred's initial.

and a rope frieze.

Corke Lodge is a house that comes into its own when Alfred Cochrane entertains. Flares are lit in the graveled forecourt to welcome guests, the house decorated with dramatic arrangements of greenery and dried flowers. Glass and silver gleam in the candlelit dining room.

Miss Georgina McGann would no doubt approve.

OPPOSITE: *Over a Regency sideboard in the dining room hangs a Grand Tour copy of an old master.*

OVERLEAF: *Detail of the mahogany chaise lounge covered with exotic striped fabric.*

A Rediscovered Clachan

The great waves of the Atlantic sweep storming on their way Shining green and silver with the hidden herring shoal.

CONSTANCE DE MARKIEVICZ, "THE WAVES OF BREFFNY"

In the remotest parts of Ireland you may still come across little groups of cottages known as *clachans*. Too small to be called villages, they are a development peculiar to Ireland; the houses are not laid out in an orderly fashion along a road or around a green but grouped higgledy-piggledy according to land tenure and preference.

The land around the *clachan* forms a distinct area known as a "town-

Only the dry stone walls provide shelter in the windswept landscape.

The studio looks out across the bay to the next headland.

Part of a bizarre collection of memorabilia: a giant stout bottle, a 1950s-style dentist's chair, and a very busty bust.

land." Near such settlements you may still see traces of "lazy beds," a method of growing potatoes used to this day in some parts of Ireland.

Many of these characteristic settlements have vanished. Mud cabins have long since returned to earth, and more permanent structures, perhaps abandoned in the famine years or through later emigration, have become heaps of stones.

Tomi and Yvonne Ungerer happened to stumble on just such a *clachan* in West Cork ten years ago. They found it just in time—only the biggest house still had a roof and the other buildings were verging on dereliction. The place had presumably been abandoned during the great exodus of the 1950s and early 1960s when people left rural Ireland for the cities or other countries.

The buildings are set on a promontory, on land kept bare of trees by the fierce southwesterlies that come roaring over the Atlantic, carrying salt spray far across the fields. A single track, or *borreen*, winding across the headland is the link with the outside world. The place is thought to have been the site of a very early settlement.

"It was there just waiting for us," says artist Tomi Ungerer.

The place did not wait in vain. A decade later all the buildings are restored, their stone walls whitewashed and the roofs tiled with traditional slate. In the interim there were eight years of back-breaking labor, much of it done by Tomi himself.

Some of the buildings now house a working farm, for Yvonne Ungerer raises sheep on their three-hundred-and-forty-acre holding while Tomi tos and fros from Germany, following his career as an internationally acclaimed cartoonist, illustrator, and writer. The farm is no amateur undertaking, but a very active business involving three hundred Texel/Suffolk cross sheep. Other buildings house a studio, guest house, and caretaker's cottage.

The biggest house—thought to have been a steward's cottage—is now the Ungerers' home. The interior treatment is simple, with an emphasis on natural materials—pine furniture, whitewashed walls, and quarry tiles under a collection of Kelim carpets providing wonderful stained-glass color. The oak-beam timbers, left exposed in the kitchen, were salvaged long ago from shipwrecks.

A conservatory has been built onto the side of the house to provide a suntrap, in which tomatoes and other tender vegetables grow sheltered from the salt winds.

Much of the pine furniture is Canadian, a legacy of the years the couple spent living in the Canadian wilderness, where Tomi wrote *Far Out Is Not Far Enough*.

Now, it seems, this ancient place of habitation at the end of Ireland is just far enough for the Ungerers.

A City Center Hideaway

At the canal bridge over our end of the street there would be life. Something to look at.

DOMINIC BEHAN, *TEEMS OF TIMES AND HAPPY RETURNS*

Not a pebble's throw from busy Leeson Street is a hidden house you might pass and never know was there. Built by leading architect Sam Stephenson, it is a place of changing levels, hanging terraces, and interesting spaces.

Where once there were two Georgian mews, the architect built a completely modern home, where he lived for nearly thirty years. The new owners, who moved there from a Georgian country home, faced the challenge of making their own imprint on such a strong architectural statement. They have succeeded admirably.

The mosaic floor in the main reception area is now given color and warmth by several magnificent Turkish Kilims. The sunken seating area is strewn with Kilim-covered cushions, the white walls now glow with a collection of eighteenth-century landscapes, and the eye is drawn to colorful bowls of dried flowers. This is essentially an evening area—beyond it sunlight streams in through windows of a gallery overlooking a small garden.

Reaching the full height of the house, this gallery has been given an Italian feeling, with stone urns filled with greenery and a cool mosaic floor contrasting a rich Kilim rug. A naive sporting picture of dogs hangs over a magnificent late Georgian settee.

Upstairs the glass, chrome, and leather furniture of the former owner has been supplanted by mahogany Georgian pieces in the dining room and by comfortable sofas and a collection of calf-bound books in the study. There is a story attached to the furniture, as there so often is in Ireland. When the couple started collecting they were taken under the wing of the Orpen brothers—colorful characters in the antiques world—who took great pride in finding pieces to suit them.

A group of Irish earthenware jars on the pine breakfast table.

OPPOSITE: A sculpture of a young boy gazes out into the garden. The Kilim is Turkish and the mahogany side table is early Georgian.

Antiques are very much a shared enthusiasm and happily one in which the couple's taste coincides completely. Some of their paintings were bought as presents to each other and many of their blue-and-white Oriental plates were finds acquired during their travels in the Far East.

The kitchen is another world, a place of cool grays and blues, with a central staircase leading to a utility room. The main work area looks onto a conservatory filled with flourishing plants and the sweet scent of jasmine and the spice of climbing geranium. It is a pleasant place to breakfast on sunny mornings. For gray days, there is a cozy room that combines a family den with an informal dining area with a pine table and dresser filled with blue dishes.

Each bedroom area is completely self-contained with bathroom en suite. The teenage daughter's room has a pretty Victorian brass bedstead and a pastel study area leading out onto its own shrub-lined terrace, while the son's room is red, white, and high tech. In the main bedroom the central skylight is exotically shaded with a Kelim. Mirrors give the room added depth, reflecting flower paintings by Irish artist Andrea Jameson and a collection

of silver-framed photographs on top of a bowfront mahogany chest of drawers.

The house, after one year's occupation, is still evolving. There are plans for a roof garden, for new furniture for the conservatory . . . but then, isn't that one of the pleasures of making a place your own?

The house is full of intriguing different levels. These steps lead down from the conservatory to the front courtyard.

OPPOSITE: *A teenage daughter's bedroom. Beyond is the pastel study area.*

Black Billy's Manor

I often wish'd that I had clear
For Life, six hundred Pounds a Year,
A handsome House to lodge a
*   Friend,*
A River at my Garden's End,
A Terras Walk and half a Rood,
Of land set out to plant a Wood.

JONATHAN SWIFT, "AN IMITATION OF THE SIXTH
SATIRE OF THE SECOND BOOK OF HORACE"

Actor Hurd Hatfield found Ballinterry House thirteen years ago when he was staying nearby. He saw a peaceful place surrounded by ancient walls and an ivy-clad house with a fanlight over the door. He continued his holiday elsewhere in Ireland but found that he could not forget the house. He has been coming back to Ballinterry ever since.

On this particular sojourn he had just reinstated a pair of first-floor windows that had been blocked up more than two hundred years ago to avoid the window tax. The northeast-facing windows of the manor house now reveal a sleepy view of the valley with the Knockmealdown and Comeragh mountains in the distance.

What scenes have been witnessed from the spot in the past Heaven alone knows, but some must have been far from peaceful. The house, parts of which may date back four hundred years, was once owned by the notorious Archdeacon "Black Billy" Ryder, instigator of the bloody 1834 Gortroe massacre, in which eleven Catholic farmers were slaughtered nearby in one of the last incidents of the Tithe Wars.

When Mr. Hatfield—whose family link with Ireland can be traced back to one Hugh Maguire, the last prince of Fermanagh, slain in battle near Cork in 1599—bought the house, it was a rabbit warren of partitions with pieces of tin hammered over the rat holes in the floor. The original chimney pieces had gone, there was no bathroom, and only one electric light.

Over the years Hurd Hatfield has restored the house. The partitions were torn down, early seventeenth-century mantelpieces were found in London and purchased for the house, and the paneled screen and fanlight that hid the handsome hall staircase were transferred to the passage leading to the library. In the old kitchen the central oak beam was uncovered and the huge fireplace, with its iron crane for holding pots and kettles over the open fire, reopened.

A tour of the house provides a fascinating odyssey through the memorabilia of the actor's distinguished career and around the history of the house and its furnishings. Often the

opposite: Every Irish house should have a horse, said the friend who donated the Mexican carousel mount. A portrait of Mr. Hatfield's great-grandmother hangs on the wall. The gold plate is a ceramic of his own making.

The ancestral portrait of Ann Winter is lit solely by Indian lamps and flanked by Chippendale chairs.

two are interlinked. In the dressing room hang the costume sketches for Hurd Hatfield's best-known role in the film adaptation of Oscar Wilde's *The Picture of Dorian Gray.* The room has a Russian theme: on a dressing table is a photograph of Czar Nicholas II and beside it an almost identical picture of Hurd playing the czar. One of Hurd's most precious possessions, a Russian teapot that belonged to Alex-

ander III, the grandfather of the last czar, stands nearby.

Everywhere there is evidence of Hurd Hatfield's creative hand. The popular eighteenth-century colors on the walls, for example, are of his own mixing, dark shades of olive and brown for the drawing room and parlor, and soft peacock green in the "Indian" room.

There is a story attached to every

possession. In the parlor is a piano, given to Hurd when his neighbor, Angela Lansbury, left Ireland. After each major film or acting part, says Mr. Hatfield, "I buy something I can't afford." A sixteenth-century tapestry hanging in the dark blue library is a reminder of his title role in the television version of *The Count of Monte Cristo.*

Fees from films enabled Hurd to add to his collection, so there are reminders of other projects in his career, which has included such roles as Pontius Pilate in *King of Kings* and Baron Rothschild in *Disraeli.* The garden is planted with trees in memory of lost friends —Michael MacLiammor, Siobhan McKenna, Yul Brynner, and most recently Geraldine Page.

One day Hurd Hatfield hopes that Ballinterry may become a study center for students who have the opportunity to travel abroad, as he once did.

LEFT: *The olive-green walls of the drawing room are a foil for a nineteenth-century naive painting.*

BELOW LEFT: *Treasures on the dressing table include an Alexander III teapot from the Winter Palace, an embroidered dancing shoe and, above, a picture of his mother proudly wheeling her new eleven-pound son.*

The new kitchen boasts a bow window brought from the United States. On the dresser is the family collection of Spode Copelandware.

A Romantic Retreat in the "Gothick" Manner

This singularly romantic spot is formed by the innermost recess of a delightful valley deeply environed by steep mountains. A newly built house erected in the glenn bespeakes the chaste taste of the Proprietor Peter La Touche but for its distinctive features it is indebted to Nature only.

So runs the flowery description on an 1803 print showing a precipitous road leading down to Lough Tay and Luggala Lodge in County Wicklow. The sentiments expressed in the caption evoke the enthusiasm of the period for scenic wonders. Fashionable taste admired all things "Gothick," a term that embraced much more than "pointed" architecture. Picturesque landscapes (the more awe inspiring, the better), ivy-clad ruins, and rustic buildings were all the rage.

In Ireland the scenery of North Wicklow and Killarney, County Kerry in particular, excited the admiration of contemporary sightseers anxious to gaze upon Nature in all her savage splendor.

The above-mentioned Peter La Touche was clearly much influenced by the Gothic notions of the period. A member of the immensely wealthy Huguenot banking family, Peter bought eight thousand acres of land in the spectacular Tay valley near Roundwood and, during the 1790s, built a Gothic-style hunting lodge overlooking the oval lake. And in this remote spot the improbability of the "cottage mansion"—a white icing-sugar fantasy with miniature battlements, crockets, and quatrefoil windows—is matched by the drama of its setting. The cascades and meanders of the Cloghogue River, the silvery sickle of beach on the south shore of the lake, the majestic mountains surrounding the valley, and the rocky escarpments reflected in the black waters of the lake must have satisfied the most Gothick of imaginations.

One Charley Carr, who lived in the Gothic-style cottage guarding the approach to Luggala Lodge, acted as a guide to the many visitors who came to admire the demesne. Local legend has it that he can still be seen walking the serpentine avenue by the lake. A print of Charley, resplendent in knee breeches and bare feet, hangs in the upstairs corridor at the Lodge.

The indefatigable Mr. and Mrs. Samuel Carter Hall, in their guide, *Hall's Ireland,* wrote in 1840, "Let no-one who visits Luggelaw [sic] without striving to make the

An early eighteenth-century upright harpsichord with gilded carving by Ferdinand Weber, who built two of these instruments in Dublin. The other is in the National Museum, Dublin. The lute, uileann pipes, and harp are part of Garech Browne's collection of musical instruments.

Pheasants strutting about near the south front of Luggala, with its miniature battlements and crockets.

The flagged entrance hall with the original "Gothick" hearth and two brass-bound turf buckets.

acquaintance of Charley Carr. . . .
Charley is of course very jealous
for the honour and glory of Luggelaw and very envious of the supe-
rior attractions of Glendalough,
which he abuses with a right good
will affirming that it is unnatural
not to love nature better than ould
stone and mortar."

Luggala Lodge was not designed
as a permanent residence but was
used for hunting parties, picnics,
and outings by the La Touche family. It was also lent to "persons of
respectability." It is quite modest
in scale, having three main reception rooms and small cottage-style
bedrooms under sloping eaves.

Luggala was subsequently bought
by Lord Powerscourt, whose lands
adjoin the estate, in the mid nineteenth century. Fifty years ago it
was sold to the Hon. Ernest Guinness, who gave it—so the story goes
—to his daughter Oonagh, Lady
Oranmore and Browne, as a wedding present.

At first the house continued to
be used much in the nineteenth-
century manner, when landed families moved seasonably among town
house, country estate, and sporting pursuits. A fortnight before the
arrival of the Oranmores, a bevy
of servants would travel over from
the family seat at Claremorris Castle to open up Luggala from May
to September.

The Speaker's clock,
made for the original
Houses of Parliament
(now the Bank of Ireland).
Beside the window is a
Victorian toy sidecar.

Later it became the permanent
home of Lady Oranmore and her
sons, Tara and Garech, and until the
late 1960s was the scene of much
entertaining and gaiety. Among the
celebrity visitors have been Bren-
dan Behan, John Huston, Burl Ives,
Sean O'Riada, and later Mick and
Bianca Jagger and Paddy Maloney
of the musical group the Chieftains.

The overflow of guests from the
main house were lodged in converted buildings still referred to
as the stables and byre. And on
one occasion the late Michael
MacLiammor was heard declaim-
ing as he went to bed, "I am going
to the cow house! The cow house!"

In its heyday Luggala had a staff of
twenty, including two, if not three,
chauffeurs. The cellar was stocked
four times a year by a Dublin wine
merchant, and a water-powered
generator was installed to provide
electricity. But as times changed,

even the Guinness fortunes were not enough to keep up the house in that manner.

Today Luggala Lodge looks just as it did in nineteenth-century paintings and sketches. Dozens of pheasants parade the parkland in front of the house. In spring the grass is covered with naturalized daffodils and deer graze beside the lake. Yet the present house is a replica of the original. For one winter night in 1956, a spark from the drawing-room fire dropped unnoticed behind the wainscot and set the room ablaze. The fire brigade was delayed on the frosty mountain road, and despite the efforts of everyone present, part of the house burned down. Lady Oranmore had it rebuilt exactly as it had been in every detail. Most of the furniture, happily, was saved.

Lady Oranmore redecorated the house, choosing for the drawing room a Gothic Revival wallpaper originally designed for the Speaker's room in the Houses of Parliament in 1860. She added elaborate floral wallpaper for the eight bedrooms under the eaves and blue for the dining room, to offset a magnificent Venetian chandelier. The house still has an agreeable

lived-in air. The bookcases overflow with books by Irish authors, harps, and *uileann* pipes, a part of Garech Browne's collection of musical instruments. Paintings by Jack Yeats and Louis le Brocquy are casually propped against other pieces of furniture.

Yet today Luggala has returned to its former role as a shooting lodge. Garech Browne and his estate manager, Robert Clotworthy, are reviving the demesne as a sporting estate. The five hundred head of deer roaming the lands are managed as a resource, and Luggala is the only Irish establishment offering the traditional gillie-led deer stalking and shooting. The old system of grouse shooting has been reinstated as well — about nine thousand pheasant are raised each year for shoots, which helps to make Luggala a self-supporting enterprise.

Last autumn saw a return to old times. All eight bedrooms in the house were occupied by a shooting party. It took two shifts of staff to cater for them. To warm the unheated house, fires were lit at 5:00 A.M. with breakfast served at 7:00. Discretion does not reveal the time at which the last port and whiskey glasses were drained.

Cottages

The traditional Irish cottage, with its links with rural folkways, is a rapidly vanishing aspect of rural Ireland. The thatched whitewashed cottages that look so romantic on picture postcards are a dwindling reminder of the past.

The layout of the long, low dwellings built of local materials reflects a legacy of tradition now all but forgotten. Typically, the old-style cottage consisted of no more than three adjoining rooms, with byres and outhouses attached. The older house often featured a front and a back door on opposite sides of the kitchen, exits and entrances being made according to the direction of the wind. Inside the floor would have been of beaten earth, with little furniture except for stools and, more recently, a dresser, table, and beds. Cooking was done over an open turf hearth, with the pot suspended over the flames on a wooden crane. Small windows were designed to minimize heat loss; the half-door was a practical solution that let in light and kept animals out.

The mill at Marybrook, framed in the doorway of the mill house.

Water and shelter from wind were prime considerations in the location of a building. There would be a spring or stream nearby and in Donegal the old custom when deciding where to build was to throw up a hat on a windy day and see where it settled.

A wooden crane over the fireplace at a Blasket Island cottage. A local chair with a string seat and milking stools provide the seating.

Cottages in rural areas are widely dispersed throughout the countryside, except in the mountains and boglands. But in the more remote areas it is still possible to see cottages built in groupings known as *clachans*. Tied by kinship, the occupants lived cooperatively, working the land according to strip cultivation, the old system used before enclosure.

But there are, of course, a great many variations on the cottage theme. There are the cottages that clustered around some point of reference—a mill or a castle—and developed into villages. There are also the estate cottages built by enlightened landowners (not all were rack-renting). Both estate cottages and those in landlord villages usually have common architectural themes. These are often much more elaborate architecturally than traditional cottages and were no doubt influenced by the British fashion for building model villages. Adare, County Limerick, with its thatched saffron-washed cottages and Caledon, County Tyrone, are both interesting examples of landlord villages.

Many of the towns and villages that developed during the eighteenth or nineteenth centuries have a ring of cottages and humbler dwellings around the grander merchants' and professionals' houses in the center. And the stepped terraces of cottages, each color-washed a different shade, that climb the sloping streets of towns and villages are one of the typical sights of Ireland.

Gate lodges, built for estate workers who oversaw the comings and goings through the main gates, are a breed all their own,

These buildings, old and new, are half hidden in an indigenous oak wood sloping down to the sea.

The conservatory at Marybrook incorporates Joseph Blair's shopfront from Church Lane, Belfast.

often reflecting in miniature the architectural mood of the "big house" they served. There are also other cottages built for specific purposes—toll houses, built for the operatives of toll gates, can still be seen by the roadside today, as can lock-keepers' dwellings beside the canal locks they served.

Cottages were also built as the playthings of the privileged. The cottage *orné* was a retreat where ladies and gentlemen could ape life's simple pleasures; such romantic cottages, set at some focal point in estate grounds, appealed to the "Gothick" tastes of the nineteenth century. Fishing and hunting lodges built for the enjoyment of Georgian and Victorian sportsmen were usually far more comfortable than the typical dwellings of the locality.

With the expansion of cities, the cottage form also came to town, adapted for those of more modest needs, as terraces of artisan dwellings or Georgian cottage-style houses with first-floor entrances over basements.

At their best, cottages can be an attractive expression of vernacular style. The use of indigenous materials, local variations in detail, and the native sense of proportion and appropriateness to setting mean that such buildings fit pleasingly into their environment. They somehow look right wherever they happen to be.

Cottages are steadily being abandoned by their original inhabitants, who regard them as damp, cramped, and dark. An abandoned cottage with the new home in front of it is a typical sight in Ireland. Some cottages are finding a new lease on life as vacation homes, and those developed by tourist interests with designs based on the traditional thatched cottage have been a resounding success.

But the Dallas-style bungalows that have superseded the cottage in rural areas are—environmentally, at least—a very poor substitute for the original.

Between Sea and Wood and Sky

*Far in a wild, unknown to public
   view,*
*From youth to age a reverend
   Hermit grew,*
*The moss his bed, the cave his
   humble cell,*
*His food the fruits, his drink the
   crystal well.*

THOMAS PARNELL, "THE HERMIT"

The rural houses in Ireland are scattered like a handful of pebbles flung across the landscape. And in contrast to the cozy village settlements of England and the rest of Europe, the cottages and farms of Ireland are often quite isolated, even hidden, far off the beaten track.

In just such a secret place in a remote part of the Kenmare Peninsula, County Kerry, a Dublin architect and his family finally found the retreat they had searched two years to find.

The force of the Atlantic winds have made it rare in Ireland to find a wood beside the sea, rarer still to find an indigenous wood of oaks and holly sloping down to a beach. The place is called *Cleanderry,* the harbor of the oakwood. At the edge of the wood was an old stone cottage, a holy place where the last

The area in front of the traditional stone cottage is paved with local slate.

The kitchen is softly lit with oil lamps and candlelight. There is a traditional dresser, a scrubbed pine table, and local rope-seat chairs.

abbot of Skellig Michael—the monastic settlement on Great Skellig, a dramatic rocky island off the Kerry coast—is said to have died in the nineteenth century. The ruins of this stone cottage became the focal point of the buildings that form the family's holiday home.

When the family discovered the spot, the 1880s house was completely dilapidated. There were trees growing out of the building

and the site was completely overgrown. A pathway had to be blasted through to allow access. Two more stone buildings were revealed once the undergrowth was cleared; these are now used for storage.

Three new buildings were designed and added by the architect. One building houses a studio; another contains bedrooms plus a living-cum-kitchen area where twenty-four people can sit down to eat. The five children and visiting friends have their own quarters. The buildings were simply executed in concrete blocks and roofed in black-painted corrugated iron. The furniture is basic, and includes traditional chairs with rope seats. Candles and oil lamps provide soft yellow light by night.

Timber floors, whitewashed walls, and stone window sills maintain the traditional cottage feeling.

The place is a paradise for holidays and long weekends. Seafood fresh from the fishermen's cooperative is a local specialty. And evening meals are regularly interrupted as the family goes out to watch the spectacular sunsets and cloud patterns over MacGillicuddy's Reeks.

Oars are propped against the gable end of one of the hundred-year-old cottages.

Blasket Island Tradition

Man to the hills, woman to the shore.

GAELIC PROVERB

The first thing artist Maria Simonds-Gooding does each morning is look from the bedroom window of her cottage across to the Great Blasket Island. The varying degrees of clarity with which the morning light reveals the outline of the island, across the three-mile stretch of sea from Dun Quinn, is a sure indication of what the weather will be like.

This forecasting method, honed through years of experience, helps to decide the pattern of her day.

Nearly twenty years ago the artist bought her stone cottage on the tip of the Dingle Peninsula from the Blasket Island man who built it. When the islander left the Blaskets in the 1950s, he brought the windows and beams from his former house with him, and built a new cottage in the traditional Blasket Island style.

The roof was of tarred canvas, just like the hull of a traditional *curragh*, and the fireside-cupboard timbers, salvaged from wrecks, are carved with the names of ships.

The cottage was bought at auction in Dingle for £810, an incredible sum of money in the 1960s. When the bidding reached a certain point, the Island man retired to the nearby chapel to light a candle. When he heard the final bid, he declared that he had been made a millionaire.

With the cottage Maria Simonds-Gooding inherited a collection of

OPPOSITE: The door of the old donkey shed.

The traditional Blasket Island cottage. The path is marked out with stones known as "Kerry diamonds," and an old-fashioned Albertina rose grows around the door. The window boxes are painted burgundy and deep blue.

The embroidered wool cushions and doll were made by Kerrywoman Ella Coffey, and the settle was made by the former owner of the cottage.

On the window sill, a collection of treasures: a picture of an icon from the Sinai monastery of St. Catherine's; three bird's eggs from a deserted nest; a painting by Michael O'Gaoithin of a funeral coming out from the Blasket Islands; and a statue that could be part of a ship's figurehead.

behind a *curragh.*

The interiors are kept simple, with whitewashed walls, local furniture, and peat-colored concrete floors. A turf fire burns in the grate and oil lamps are lit in the evenings, although the cottage now has electricity.

Some of Maria's most prized possessions are the wonderfully colorful cushions and dresses made for her by Ella Coffey. Their paths first crossed at the Puck Fair, the three-day festival of drinking and music at Killorglin that culminates in the crowning of a billy goat, or Puck. Ella, who comes from the "Bull Ring" in Tralee, was there drinking and dancing and wearing a dress of many colors made from nun's veiling embroidered with rainbow wools. Asked if she might make a similar one for Maria, Ella said if she went off the drink for six weeks she would.

And so she did.

Dun Quinn is known as "the last parish before America." Maria Simonds-Gooding stays there for about half the year, working hard and living very simply, sometimes crossing to Blaskets to work there, living on fish caught from the rocks and snared rabbits. She has an etching press and painting instruments in her studio; the bare lines

holy pictures, which still hang there, and a wooden settle made by the Blasket Island man. Slates were placed over the tarred roof, the floors of the cottage lowered by a foot to bring in more light, and French drains dug to deal with the problem of damp. Over the years a bedroom and a studio have been added, tucked at the back of the house to preserve the cottage's traditional appearance.

The green-painted wooden crane over the fire came from the local writer Peig Sayer's cottage, and was given to Maria by her son Michael O'Gaoithin, the poet. Some of Michael's paintings also hang in the cottage, showing traditional scenes from Blasket Island life—a seal hunt, a funeral procession coming out from the islands, and a cow being towed across to the islands

OPPOSITE: The cottage is furnished with local pieces. By the door is an old grindstone found when the cottage was being built. The walls are hung with holy pictures and a statue of the Virgin from Mexico City. On the left is the edge of one of the last spinning wheels from the Blasket Islands. Fishing lines hang on the rafters.

and stone-walled fields of the surrounding landscape provide the subject matter for her work.

For the rest of the year she works in Dublin, bringing her work for exhibition in London and New York and traveling to find new sources of inspiration for her paintings.

But wherever she is Maria is always conscious of her Kerry home, secure in the knowledge that the islands, the sea, and the wild countryside are there to provide energy and inspiration for her work.

The Past Recaptured

Soon after entering the county of Down we began to feel we were in another country, in a district at least where the habits as well as the looks of the people were altogether different from those to which we had been accustomed.

MR. AND MRS. SAMUEL CARTER HALL,
HALLS IRELAND

One of the loveliest sights in Northern Ireland used to be the fields of flax in bloom, lakes of sky-blue flowers rippling in the wind. From those fields grew the linen industry, once the pride of Ulster. The knowledge involved in transforming the fibrous flax plant into the finest linen has now virtually passed into folk memory.

But at Marybrook Mill in County Down, some of the old skills are being revived.

As the road dips and rises over the egg-shaped drumlins of Down, you can catch a glimpse of the mill complex, cradled in a curve of the swift-flowing Ballinahinch River. A

A traditional cottage chimney breast, complete with an iron crane on which pot and kettle hung over the flames. A gilded ceiling rose hangs over the mantel; the oil lamp is from a church in Glencolumbkille, County Donegal.

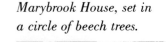

Marybrook House, set in a circle of beech trees.

The back staircase. Beside it is a Lambeg drum, the traditional Orange drum featured in Twelfth of July parades, complete with portrait of William of Orange. It was discovered in Johnston's drum shop, Belfast.

The doorway to the mill. The original weights are still used for the grain scales.

Scottish planter family by the name of Silcock became tenants of the land at Marybrook and in the early eighteenth century built a small flax-scutching mill there. By the mid nineteenth century they had added a corn mill, a new flax mill, and a two-story miller's house. The two-hundred-acre holding was a flourishing hive of industry, with thirteen *bothys,* or cottages, on the land as well as a warehouse for making linen handkerchiefs, employing sixty local women. But the hustle and bustle was stilled fifty years ago. Silcock, the last of that family to live at Marybrook, suffered a bout of influenza and took to his fireside chair. The mill wheels ground no more and the place became neglected.

The neglect of Marybrook was probably the saving of the place. The house was hidden by laurel, gorse, and an eight-foot ash heap; the roof leaked, the floors had rotted, and the furniture had been vandalized. But when John and Sheila Lewis-Crosbie found Marybrook, the corn and scutching mills were intact and virtually in working order, a tribute to the enduring skills of the Ulstermen who built them nearly one hundred and forty years ago.

At the time John Lewis-Crosbie was director of the National Trust in Northern Ireland. He had been searching for a flax mill on behalf of the Trust with a view to restoring

The mill wheel powers the rollers of the McAdam flax breaker.

an example of Ulster's rapidly vanishing heritage.

As things turned out, the Lewis-Crosbies eventually took on the project themselves, moving there in 1973. The house and mill were restored on a shoestring budget, with Sheila and John doing a lot of the work themselves. Many of the materials were salvaged from condemned buildings—the eighteenth-century paneling came from a house in Molesworth Street, Dublin. The maple flooring came from a former ballroom in Belfast, and huge Oregon pine trusses were saved from the demolition of the Queen Victoria School, Belfast.

This pine was originally brought from America as ballast on the emigration ships that carried thousands

The drawing room in the new wing. Its floor was salvaged from a Belfast ballroom, and the fireplace from Molesworth Street, Dublin. The silver table behind the sofa is George III.

of Irish people to the States in the grim post-famine years. When the pine was sawed into flooring planks for the Lewis-Crosbies' drawing room, it seemed as full of resin as the day it was felled over a century ago.

The Lewis-Crosbies built a new wing, which houses the drawing room and main bedroom and links the Silcock's original cottage to the mill house. Ingenious use has been found for other architectural waifs. A former shopfront from Joseph Blair's of Church Lane, Belfast, has been incorporated into a sunny conservatory connecting the house and the former warehouse, which has been converted into offices for John.

The range in the former kitchen was replaced with the traditional grate, complete with cooking crane, from the two-room cottage that predated the mill house. Interestingly, the bars on the fire are vertical, not horizontal, indicating that it was probably used to burn the *shoughs*, or woody outer part of the flax.

One of the biggest undertakings in the restoration was the rebuilding of the clay and stone weir, which had been breached by a bulldozer. The work, which included dredging the mill pond and clearing out the "races" that channeled the water to drive the mill wheel, was carried out with help from Voluntary Service International workers.

Reinstating parts of the century-and-a-half-old technology was a challenge. As John Lewis-Crosbie points out, "There is no one left now who will tell you the exact angle at which to put water into the buckets of the mill wheel." The missing cockannie, or weathervane, that once topped the drying grain was another puzzle. Research led to a cockannie atop a mill that was about to be demolished in County Tyrone, and to a former miller in nearby Killinchey who unraveled the mystery of its installation.

The mill is now earning its keep, producing stone-ground flour for a local bakery. Water once again drives the flax mill and the dash churn, which has ingeniously been linked to the water power. And the eel trap that was part of the complex once more catches eels as they journey from the Sargasso Sea upstream in early autumn to breed. The forty-acre farm now provides grazing for Sheila Lewis-Crosbie's growing herd of pedigree Simenthal cattle.

Flax is being grown on an experimental basis by nearby friends, and the skills involved in breaking and scutching the flax are being rediscovered—partly through the local historical society. And in this particular quiet corner of County Down, part of Ulster's heritage is being brought back to life.

Castles and Strongholds

Surely the most fascinating of all dwelling places is the castle, and Ireland has a unique variety and number of them. Steeped in atmosphere and history, they range from stern, square keeps guarding isolated sweeps of countryside to the romantic Gothic Revival castles of the Victorian era.

Irish castles index the march of history through the centuries. The earliest fortified dwellings in Ireland were the Iron Age hill forts, or *duns,* wherein entire hilltops were enclosed with walls and ditches. Ring forts, promontory forts, and *crannogs*—lake island forts—were variations on the theme. Many traces of these early defensive constructions can still be found.

Rich green velvet bed hangings.

The more familiar stone-built castles were introduced to Ireland by Anglo-Normans after the invasion of 1169. The earlier Norman castles were of the *motte*-and-bailey variety—wooden buildings above a mound with a ditch and palisade around the base. Traces of these mounds are still in evidence. The Normans rapidly overran three-quarters of the country and began to build more permanent fortresses to consolidate their conquest.

A medieval Spanish Vargena, originally used by monks as a kind of filing cabinet, stands in the grand hall at Castle Leslie. Behind it hangs an early eighteenth-century painting of scenes from a chase held at a Hapsburg hunting lodge.

Norman castles vary from simple stone towers, usually surrounded by a *bawn* or protective wall, to large complexes with elaborate defense systems. Usually built on a vantage point overlooking the surrounding country or strategic landing places, such fortresses have dramatic settings.

The majority of castles are concentrated in the southwest of Ireland. And the sight of a ruined tower standing on top of a hill is a particularly characteristic sight in counties Limerick, Cork, Galway, and Tipperary.

Some indication of the popularity and necessity of castle dwelling in ancient and medieval times can be gathered by the fact that about three thousand castles or forts were built in Ireland between 1169 and the seventeenth century.

The defensive architecture that continued to be built throughout the Middle Ages includes a variety of forms. A tower, or stronghouse, was the typical home of a person of substance and had three to five floors, with the family living on the upper floors. More complicated fortresses had all kinds of defensive features—barbicans, drawbridges, battlements, tower turrets, and "murder holes," through which projectiles or boiling liquid could be dropped on attackers.

Castles and tower houses were still being built during the sixteenth and even the seventeenth centuries—a reminder of the troubled state of the country. Planters who came to Ireland in this period also built fortified homes; those built in Ulster are still referred to as "plantation castles."

By the end of the seventeenth century the gentry began to abandon their castles and to build more comfortable houses, often beside or attached to the old forts. And as classical ideals and Palladianism began to gain influence, castles became regarded as distinctly old-fashioned.

But inevitably the wheel of fashion turned full circle, and by 1790 castles had become the inspiration for the "Gothick" style that was an expression of the Romantic period. These castles were a great deal more comfortable than their predecessors. Often medieval revival designs simply included such elements of "Gothick" architecture as decorative features with battlements, turrets, and fan vaulting. Existing Georgian houses were often given the "Gothick" treatment with the addition of crenelations or towers. But complete mock castles were also built. Charleville Forest and Luttrellstown (illustrated in this chapter) are fine examples of Georgian castles.

The Victorians, too, were inspired by medieval architecture, with Gothic Revival castles becoming the rage as classical mansions came to be seen as old hat. Enthusiasm for the medieval and baronial styles ran to quite extraordinary lengths, and architects included all kinds of authentic details from dungeons to bartizans.

Castles are one of the most dramatic architectural features in Ireland. Many are ruined and derelict, some are being protected against further dilapidation by the Board of Works, and a few are still homes. A number of Irish castles are now open to the public for touring or as guest houses or hotels, so that it is possible to sample the splendors of the past with all the comforts of the twentieth century.

Below stairs at Castle Leslie. Each of the twenty-nine bells has a different tone.

Dreaming by the Lakeside

Glaslough with rows of books upon
its shelves
Written by Leslies all about
themselves.

JONATHAN SWIFT

A coat of arms with the motto *Grip Fast* suggests a degree of tenacity in the family who bears it. And, indeed, the phrase appears very appropriate in the case of the Leslies of Glaslough.

A Leslie ancestor acquired the maxim after 1067, in acknowledgment of his role as protector of St. Margaret of Scotland. His armorial bearings feature three buckles, the two extra buckles (in addition to the normal one of a postillion rider) being used to help the blessed Margaret hang onto his steed while fleeing.

The family's Irish fortunes were founded by an equally tenacious gentleman in the seventeenth century. John Leslie pursued a successful career in the Church and was made Bishop of the Isles in Scotland and later Bishop of Raphoe, one of the Irish sees. He built an Episcopal palace there and defended it successfully against the Cromwellians. When news of the Restoration came in 1660, Bishop Leslie rode to London at the ripe old age of eighty. A grateful Charles asked him to become Archbishop of Canterbury in recognition of his loyalty to the crown, but he turned down the offer and accepted instead two thousand guineas, an enormous sum in those times.

The bishop purchased a large estate at Glaslough in County Monaghan, retired from office, married, and lived to father a sizeable family. Around 1664, he built one of the typical stronghouses of the period beside Glaslough Lake, the tower of which was later incorporated into a pleasant Dutch gabled mansion by Leslie descendants.

In 1870 another John Leslie (who refused a viscountcy saying it was vulgar to become a peer as late as the nineteenth century and settled

The conservatory, once filled with flowering hothouse plants. The seat is a copy of Nero's throne.

Castle Leslie, with its magnificent lakeside setting.

Among the collection of miniatures in the drawing room are Sir John Leslie, fourth baronet of Glaslough; his sister, Mary Crawshay; Mrs. Henry Clay Ide, godmother of Desmond Leslie; and HRH the Duke of Connaught, Queen Victoria's youngest son.

instead for a baronetcy), inspired by his travels on the European Grand Tour, determined to build an Italianate villa overlooking Glaslough Lake as a love nest for his beautiful young bride. In the last half of the eighteenth and first half of the nineteenth century, the education of gentlemen of refinement was not complete without the tour. Thus, the classical architecture of Italy and Greece became a major influence on the architecture of the period.

Sir John engaged the Ulster architects Sir Charles Lanyon and William Henry Lynn to carry out the work, and the old house was subsequently demolished. Some of his dreams materialized in the magnificent Renaissance-style interiors—where his own influence can be seen—and in the cloister, an exact copy of Michelangelo's design for Santa Maria delgi Angeli in Rome.

But at some point in the execution of the house, which was built over eighteen months, Sir John went away, leaving the exterior design to Lynn. The result belongs to the Belfast brick palace school, though it is somewhat redeemed by the magnificent lakeside setting.

Sir John apparently stood outside his new home fuming, "But that is not what I *meant*," having learned the salutary lesson never to go away when the builders are in. He evidently became reconciled to the

appearance of his new home, for the vestibule bears the legend *Dulce Domum* (sweet home), and is adorned with plaques of the heads of his four children. And the mosaic floor of the entrance hall—after an original in Pompeii—features the doves of peace.

The principal rooms are the barrel-vaulted great hall, featuring Ionic columns in *scagliola*, the drawing and dining rooms, which overlook enchanting views of the lake, and the imposing staircase hall. Here, Sir John's hand is very much in evidence. Classical statuary brought back from his Italian travels stands under the Romanesque arches of the gallery, which runs around two sides of the stairwell and is hung with many of Sir John's portrait studies. The part of the long gallery that extends behind the cloister also features frescoes in the Pre-Raphaelite manner painted by Sir John, a talented artist and Royal Academician.

His son—yet another Sir John—married a beautiful American, Leonie Jerome, whose sister became Lady Randolph Churchill. The young Winston Churchill frequently visited his aunt and uncle at Castle Leslie as they entertained fashionable Edwardian society. Illustrious guests included Queen Margaret of Sweden, the Duke of Connaught (Queen Victoria's youngest son), and Prince Pierre de Monaco (Prince Rainier's father).

Generations of independent-minded Leslies stare from the walls. There is Dean Charles Leslie, known as the "choleric cleric," of whom his contemporary Dr. Samuel Johnson observed, "Leslie is a reasoner against whom it is difficult to reason." In the great hall hangs a portrait of the formidable Clara Jerome, known as the "Red Indian ancestress" because of her Iroquois blood, who intervened in the looting of the Tuileries during the French Commune, salvaging pieces that she had wheeled back to her hotel in a barrow.

A strong literary leaning runs through the family. Jonathan Swift, dean of Christ Church and author of *Gulliver's Travels,* used to visit Robin and Harry Leslie and wrote the mischievous verse quoted earlier. Sir Shane Leslie continued the tradition and wrote twenty books, while his son, Desmond Leslie, author of *The Flying Saucers Have Landed,* is currently working on his tenth novel. Castle Leslie is owned jointly by Desmond and his brother, Sir John, who lives in Rome while Desmond is the current Leslie in residence.

Castle Leslie was built with every modern convenience of the day and is a monument to the ingenuity of Victorian technology. There is a

Old Sir John's bedroom.

hand-operated elevator, used to carry visitors' baggage to the upper floors, a speaking tube—the forerunner of the house telephone—and the first-ever gas stove in Ireland. The plumbed bathroom was also a first, and a massive boiler provided heat for the reception rooms and the hothouse.

The Leslie estate was originally one of the largest in these islands, with thirty thousand acres around Glaslough and a further thirty thousand acres in Donegal, providing work for hundreds of people. It was featured in the first page of a nineteenth-century book on great landowners. Glaslough is a charming example of a model estate village with a common architectural theme, built by philanthropic Leslies for their tenants.

The baronial-style entrance hall. The mosaic floor is based on an original at Pompeii.

But now Castle Leslie is stripped of the estates that once supported it. Under the Wyndam Acts, the land was redistributed to tenants by the Land Commission; today, Castle Leslie retains only the twelve-hundred-acre demesne enclosed

by a five-mile estate wall. The family no longer owns the village, which was sold to tenants after the Leslies set the rents at an ill-considered two shillings and sixpence, though the Leslies themselves had to pay three shillings per unit plus repairs.

Today the basement at Glaslough is empty. The walled gardens are leased to a nurseryman, the stables to an equestrian center, and the billiard room is used by Desmond Leslie's son as a workshop to build speaker systems that have won awards. But the house and the Leslies remain a testimony on the one hand to the durability and quality of Victorian architecture and to family tradition on the other.

A panel throne—once a necessity for bishops, in the event that the pope dropped in—which was bought by the second baronet. Above hangs a portrait of a Spanish infanta.

Entertaining in the Grand Manner

At about 4 o'clock Hans Hamilton and I set out in a post chaise which we hired for the occasion and drove to Luttrellstown to Lord Carhampton . . . it was near 7 o'clock before the whole company which was computed to amount to about 230 people were assembled, when we went to dinner which was laid out in a great many different rooms.

FROM THE DIARY OF ANDREW HAMILTON, 1796

Surrounded by one of the finest demesnes in the country, the peace and parkland of Luttrellstown Castle seems so remote as to belong to another world. Yet the estate lies just four miles from the heart of Dublin beyond Phoenix Park, which keeps the city at bay.

The earliest mention of the Luttrells is in the time of King John, in the early thirteenth century. Sir Jeffrey Luttrell was one of his loyal band of Anglo-Norman knights and one of the rooms at Luttrellstown is known as "King John's chamber." The first definite connection between the king and the Luttrell family, however, according to Desmond Fitzgerald, Knight of Glin, is a mention of the seizure of the estate on the death of Robert Luttrell in 1436.

The family became one of the leading dynasties of the Pale, the triangle in the southeast where English rule held sway. As were many Anglo-Irish estates, Luttrellstown was confiscated during the Commonwealth, but Thomas Luttrell was reinstated following the restoration of Charles II to the throne in 1660. There then followed three generations of Luttrells infamous

The dining room features Rococo-style plasterwork and a Dutch painted ceiling by Jacob de Wit. The chairs are George III. The cartouche frames an Aubusson tapestry.

The staircase hall was redesigned in the eighteenth-century manner by Felix Harbord.

The castellated and turreted "Gothick" front encloses a medieval castle.

for their evildoing and treachery.

As is the case with many Irish houses, the architectural history of Luttrellstown is as complex as the story of its owners. The estate progressed from stronghold, through manor and classic stages, to "Gothick" and Tudor Revival and finally back to nineteenth-century Gothic Revivalism.

Part of the medieval castle remains and is now distinguishable by steep spiral staircases and enormously thick walls. The Hearth Lists of 1664—houses at that time were taxed according to number of fireplaces—shows Luttrellstown as one of the largest houses in the Dublin area, with twelve hearths.

The present exterior is a typical example of a mock castle created in response to the fashionable enthusiasm for things "Gothick" that swept Britain and Ireland from the end of the eighteenth century. There seems to be some uncertainty among experts as to whether Lord Carhampton or Luke White was responsible for encasing the old castle in a Romantic "Gothick" exterior with battlements and turrets.

When the interiors of the V-shaped castle were remodeled, the ballroom was given a vaulted ceiling with Adamesque plasterwork. An octagonal entrance hall in the Gothic style was also added at the time. Further "improvements"—including a Tudor Revival dining hall—were made, probably by Luke White's fourth son, who became Lord Annaly.

The Annalys left Luttrellstown in the 1900s, and the castle was rented to various people before being bought by the Hon. Ernest Guinness in 1927 as a wedding gift to his daughter, Eileen Plunkett.

During Mrs. Plunkett's reign, Luttrellstown underwent a further transformation. The magnificently gloomy Tudor banqueting hall was replaced by architect and interior designer Felix Harbord with a dining room in the Baroque style, with festooned and eagled plasterwork and a Dutch painted ceiling by Jacob de Wit. The staircase hall was also redone in the grand manner, a magnificent painted ceiling

One of the fourteen guest rooms, furnished with a George III mahogany fourposter bed with an arched canopy.

Detail of the plasterwork in the dining room, designed by Felix Harbord and featuring eagles and swags.

The alcove in the servery displays hand-painted Longchamps plates.

by James Thornhill was introduced, and a mantelpiece and overmantle became a fitting setting for Gerrit Van Honthorst's full-length portrait of Charles II.

In this very splendid setting Mrs. Plunkett entertained in great style. Prince Rainier and Princess Grace of Monaco and David Niven numbered among a guest list that featured both royalty and celebrities. The hospitality and comfort of Luttrellstown were legendary—a reminder of a more gracious age.

Today, Luttrellstown continues to offer hospitality, albeit in a slightly different vein. In 1984 the property was bought by the Primwest Consortium and refurbished as a luxurious residence for hire by private individuals or for use as a conference center.

Dry rot and other problems were discovered, leading the architects, Brian O'Halloran and Associates, and the contractors to spend two-and-a-half years and over £2 million restoring the fabric of the house, replacing doors, windows, and detailing down to the bolection moldings. The somewhat antediluvian kitchens have been replaced by a country-style kitchen with pine fittings, serveries, and a breakfast room furnished in dark oak.

Many of the more important pieces of furniture were bought by the present owners and augmented by a fine collection of eighteenth-century furniture. The entire castle has been refurbished, and while the reception rooms retain their original form, the bedrooms have been altered to provide bathrooms en suite, many of them featuring miracles of nineteenth-century bath technology.

A glance at the visitors' book shows that celebrities are still welcomed at Luttrellstown. And in its new lease on life the castle seems set to continue the long tradition of glittering hospitality that began over three hundred years ago.

The magnificent copper hip bath in the principal bedroom was made by the French firm Charles Andre, and has its own patent water heater.

Gothick Fantasy

What if the glory of escutcheoned
    doors,
And buildings that a haughtier
    age designed,
The pacing to and fro on polished
    floors,
Amid great chambers and long
    galleries, lined
With famous portraits of our
    ancestors;
What if those things the greatest
    of mankind
Consider most to magnify, or to bless,
But take our greatness with our
    bitterness?

WILLIAM BUTLER YEATS, "ANCESTRAL HOUSES"

From an endless driveway winding lazily through parkland and oakwoods the towers of Charleville Forest appear to shift mysteriously. Each bend reveals a different aspect, a massive castellated block, a square tower with pinnacles, a slender tower rising above the incredible silhouette.

The final approach is dramatic, the building suddenly revealed beyond a thick oakwood—a fantasy castle that might have been drawn from the pages of a fairy tale. The huge corbelled arch over the doorway and the massive bulk of the cutstone castle are almost intimidating in their magnificent scale.

Charleville Forest, one of the finest Irish examples of a full-blown Georgian castle in the medieval revival style.

But then, Charleville was designed to impress in every way. Built from 1800 for Charles Bury, first earl of Charleville, the architect Francis Johnston's masterpiece is an exercise in "Gothick" splendor.

The interior of Charleville is every bit as impressive as its exterior. In the hall, a wide flight of stairs rises to the *piano nobile* under a groined ceiling carried on graceful columns. At the top stands an intricately paneled doorway under an inverted ogee arch; beyond is the breathtaking gallery.

This vast room runs the entire length of the central block and is dominated by a plaster fan-vaulted ceiling with an enormous row of pendants running down the middle. Every detail is in the Gothic style—the two fireplaces with carved paneling reaching to the ceiling and the matching side tables between the windows. The room looks out over a formal garden of Florence Court yews planted in the shape of a half Union Jack.

The other principal reception rooms lie on either side of the main staircase. The dining room has a coffered ceiling and a Gothic dado. The ceiling was painted in the 1860s by the Arts and Crafts designer William Morris. Charleville was the only house Morris decorated in Ireland.

OVERLEAF LEFT: *A view of the long gallery, which was restored and refurnished by Michael McMullan. The fan-vaulted ceiling was inspired by Winchester Cathedral. The framed tapestry dates from 1840, and the Irish gilt sofas are nineteenth century.*

OVERLEAF RIGHT: *Gothic splendor in the dining room. The chairs are Jacobean-style Victorian pieces; the fireplace was based on the design of the chapel doorway at Magdalene College, Oxford.*

Ironically, Charleville was built at one of the economic turning points in Irish history—the Act of Union in 1800—and the construction was followed by an inevitable decline in the family fortunes. In 1875 the title died with the fifth earl of Charleville and the estate passed to the female line. The Bury family last lived in the castle in 1912—Charles Howard, who inherited, preferred to live in his other home at Belvedere in Mullingar. In the 1920s the castle was occupied for a time by the Irish Free State army and the furniture was sold off in 1947.

After the castle was abandoned in the 1960s, it was vandalized, its windows were smashed, and the process of dereliction began. But for one of those extraordinary quirks of fate, the future of Charleville Castle would have been bleak.

By chance, Michael McMullan, who lived in London at the time, saw an advertisement for a banking firm in which Charleville Forest was featured as Dracula's bank. Intrigued, he tracked down its whereabouts, came to Ireland, and on the basis of what he saw arranged a repairing lease with the Bury descendants, who still own the castle. And in 1971, with great energy and enthusiasm, Mr. McMullan set about restoring the castle as a setting for his collection of furniture.

Work that had previously been done by an army of servants and craftsmen was an immense undertaking for one person. It took three months alone to paint the ceiling of the gallery, and sixty rolls of paper to cover its walls.

The huge rooms were completely refurnished with a combination of family pieces and auction buys. A series of magnificent chandeliers and light fittings, made in Hydrabad in India and assembled by Michael, were added. The atmosphere of an ancestral home has been recreated in every detail with paintings, ceramics, and artifacts. Mr. McMullan even made the curtains for the huge Gothic windows.

The reception rooms of the castle were opened to visitors, who were entertained to tea and given a guided tour for a small fee, but the experiment has not been an unqualified success. A shadow has fallen on the relationship between the occupant of the castle and some of the people of the nearby town. It is to be hoped that a benign fate will take a hand in the future to ensure that Johnston's exuberant "Gothick" fantasy loses neither its enchantment nor its benefactor.

The music room and morning room. Gilded caryatids glitter on the chandeliers, which were made for the Nizam of Hydrabad, India. The sofa is an Irish piece made in Limerick in 1910.

Island Enchantment

A winding stair, a chamber arched
  with stone,
A grey stone fireplace with an open
  hearth,
A candle and a written page.

WILLIAM BUTLER YEATS, "MY HOUSE"

The oak chair is Arts and Crafts, and the cabinet limed oak.

Lambay Island may lie just fifteen miles north of Dublin, but its timeless enchantment belongs to another world. On the seaward side of the island, high cliffs fall from Pilot's Hill and Heath Hill, a buttress against the east wind. The sheltered western side slopes gently to a silvery beach.

The magic of the island has attracted a varied succession of inhabitants down through the centuries. It is reputed to have been the site of an early Christian monastery, founded by St. Columba in the sixth century and later sacked by Vikings. Pirates used it as a base from which to plunder the shipping of Dublin Bay. A unique defensive tower and fortress built in 1473 marks its strategic importance in history.

Island dwellings are very much part of Irish tradition, since surrounding water helps to provide a perfect natural defense. *Crannogs,* or island dwellings on lakes, were used by the Celts, and many of the early

View of the castle framed in the gateway through the curtain wall that encircles and shelters the grounds.

Christian monasteries were built on islands. More recently, part of the attraction of island dwelling is the privacy it allows and Lambay, for all its proximity to Dublin, remains a private, secret place.

In 1904 the Hon. Cecil Baring, later Lord Revelstoke, and his beautiful young wife saw an advertisement with the legend "Island up for sale with rabbits and coast

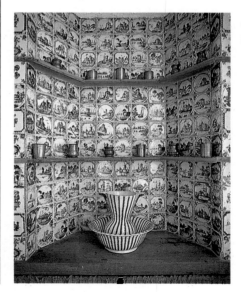

Dutch tiles line an alcove in the bathroom.

A splay-legged Arts and Crafts stool in the linen-hung bathroom.

guards." It was the start of a love affair with the mile-square island that was to last their lifetimes. And when they brought their friend Edwin Lutyens, the eminent English architect, to Lambay, he too fell under its spell. Using the rare gray-green porphyry rock of the island and incorporating the old fortress, he created a romantic retreat for the couple.

Today Lambay Castle remains exactly as Edwin Lutyens designed and furnished it in collaboration with Mrs. Baring. This masterpiece is one of the two Irish houses he designed; the other, now a hotel, is at Renvyle in Connemara. Lutyens is perhaps best known for his British country houses, his imperial buildings in New Delhi, and for his collaboration with the great garden designer Gertrude Jekyll. But of all his work Lambay Castle has the most dramatic setting.

Lutyens's design for the oak stairrail. The finials are capped with an obelisk-and-ball design.

The castle is made all the more fascinating by the way Lutyens's plan reveals itself to visitors as a series of surprises. From the sea the castle remains mysterious, hidden by mist, its gray-green stone camouflaged by a wood growing within the massive curtain wall. From the pier a series of terraces designed by Lutyens leads gently upward, but the castle remains hidden behind the encircling walls that shelter growing plants and trees.

The approach leads past a row of whitewashed Coast Guard cottages across velvety sheep-shorn

Long corridors and passageways linking the different sections of the castle add to the mystery of what lies 'round the corner.

The drawing room, a part of the old fort. On the table is a bowl of island birds' eggs. The chairs are upholstered in the "butcher's-blue" linen favored by Lutyens.

grass. Suddenly, there is a dramatic vista of a bastioned gateway, framing an avenue of grass and revealing beyond the castellated gables and mullioned windows of Lambay Castle.

Perhaps because the castle is approached only on foot, there is no main front door but rather a choice of minor side doors. These open onto passages that heighten the sense of expectation, of revelations to follow.

Lutyens modified the old fort with its crenellated gables and attached a new wing, built around a courtyard and steeply roofed in Dutch pantiles, to the old building. He linked the two with an underground passage. From the air the plan looks simple, but inside the impression is of labyrinthine passages with the unexpected at every turn—here a spiral stone staircase, there

OPPOSITE: *Razorbills— some of the island residents.*

RAZORBILL

Why did the Razorbill raise her bill?
Because the Sea-urchin wanted to see 'er chin!

Silverware in a niche in the dining room.

The oak dresser in the dining room holds a collection of delft plates, including the "Merry Man" series.

The dining-room sideboard, set with silver chafing dishes.

OPPOSITE: *The vaulted dining room, with furniture in native elm and limed oak. Kilims glow against the scrubbed elm floorboards.*

The bed and cupboards in the principal dressing room were designed by Lutyens. The chintzes are the originals.

a glimpse of the vaulted drawing room, next a doorway opening onto a vista of terraces built to a forced perspective, which gives an illusion of distance.

Characteristically, Lutyens used local materials. He took the island's own porphyry and limestone from a nearby quarry to frame the mullioned windows, for the great stone fireplaces, and as flags for paving. Indigenous wood—beech, oak, elm, and sycamore—were used for furniture. Throughout the house, whitewashed walls, unvarnished elm floors, scrubbed pale silver, and stone are a neutral foil to the colors of Oriental rugs and collections of English delftware displayed around the house.

Each window offers a totally different view—among them, an inner courtyard where the pantiled roof swoops down nearly to the ground; a whole series of perspectives created by the terraces and walls of the garden: the trees and daffodils that flourish inside the shelter of the curtain wall.

Although the house was completed in 1910, work on the garden and the surrounding walls continued until the 1930s. Lutyens was a family friend and frequent visitor to the island. He was godfather to the present Lord Revelstoke. In the albums, which are a tribute to Rupert Revelstoke's considerable skill as a photographer, there is a photo captioned "Uncle Ned," picturing Lutyens puffing contentedly on his habitual briar pipe.

Much of the furniture in the house was discovered by Mrs. Baring in the days before such pieces became fashionable: Samarkand and Bokhara rugs, oak and pine dressers, tables, and cabinets. The simplicity of line in furniture, the use of unvarnished native woods, and the collections of pottery give the rooms a curiously contemporary feel.

Rupert Revelstoke's nostalgic sepia-tinted photographs hanging on the billiard-room walls record the wildlife of the island. Puffins, razorbills, guillemots, sheerwaters, and gulls provide eggs that are still collected and sold as a specialty to a Dublin delicatessan. There have been attempts to introduce other more exotic forms of life on Lambay, including mouflons, fallow deer, and wallabies, but few have prospered—almost as though the island accepts only rightful inhabitants on its shores.

BELOW AND BELOW RIGHT: Part of the charm of Lutyens's plan lies in the series of contrasting vistas.

OVERLEAF LEFT: Simplicity and the use of local native woods were the hallmark of Lutyens's furniture designs.

OVERLEAF RIGHT: The spectacular limestone fireplace in the main bedroom. The fourposter bed, designed by Lutyens, has hangings made by Lady Revelstoke.

Index

Design
J. C. Suarès

Paul Zakris

Composed in Bodoni Book by
Arkotype Inc., New York,
New York
Printed and bound by
Toppan Printing Company, Ltd.,
Tokyo, Japan